**DEVELOPMENT OF THE
ENGLISH BOOK TRADE
1700-1899**

JOHN NICHOLS, ESQ. F.S.A.

Author of the History of Leicestershire Literary Anecdotes; &c.&c.
and Editor of the Gentleman's Magazine.

Born 1745. ___ Died 1826.

John Nichols in old age

DEVELOPMENT OF THE ENGLISH BOOK TRADE, 1700-1899

edited by
Robin Myers
and
Michael Harris

Oxford Polytechnic Press

Publishing Pathways Series

Colin Ridler, Out-house Publishing (out of print)

Toyohiko Yoshizaki, Publishing East and West

1st Impression 1981

2nd Impression 1982

3rd Impression 1982

Development of the English book trade, 1700-1899.
—(Publishing pathways series; 3)
1. Book industries and trades—Great Britain
—History—Congresses
I. Myers, Robin   II. Harris, Michael
III. Series
338.4'7686'0941   Z325

ISBN 0-902692-26-7

Oxford Polytechnic Press 1981

ISBN 0 902692 26 7

Printed and bound at Oxford Polytechnic,

Headington, Oxford OX3 OBP

Contents

Preface

The papers in this volume were presented at a conference
organised by the University of London Department of Extra-Mural
Studies. This was the second bibliographical conference run by
the Department and it was held at 26 Russell Square on Saturday
22 November and Sunday 23 November 1980, with Robin Myers
in the chair. The third conference will be on Saturday 5 December
and Sunday 6 December 1981 and the subject will be Book
Distribution and Sales in England from 1700. The six speakers
will include Giles Barber on trade with the Continent, Michael
Harris on the publication of trials and legal proceedings in the
eighteenth century, Ian Maxted on books and readers in the West
Country, and Robin Myers on George Henry Robins, Regency
auctioneer. It is hoped that the conference will become an annual
event at which various themes related to current research in the
field will be considered. This publication marks a step towards
this objective and our thanks are due to the Publishing Course of
the Oxford Polytechnic who have made it possible. Tom Colverson
has been the guiding spirit throughout, unstinting in putting his
publishing experience at our disposal and tireless in his enthusiasm.
His colleagues, Laura Cohn and Keith Vaughan, and his Course

students, Graham Russel and Jeremy Trevathan, have worked
hard to see the publication through. The circumstances of publication by OPP, where each book is carried out by one generation
of students, has meant that there was scant time for re-checking
of references. The editors apologise for any inaccuracies or
inconsistencies on this account, as they do for any incorrect
listing of names of professions of those who attended the conference.

Our opening speaker was to have been Ian Parsons, the Chair-
man of Chatto and Windus; we counted ourselves particularly
fortunate to number among our contributors one so well equipped
in every way- a lifelong publisher, an historian by training and
a particularly witty and lucid lecturer. 'The Backward Look' at
publishing, which was the subject of his Stationers' Company
Livery Lecture for 1979, showed him an authority on copyright
history. He would have explained the dates in the original title
of our conference (1709-1899), and would have described book
trade legislation from the first Copyright Act of 1709 to that of
1884, the Stamp Act of 1712 (later dealt with by Alan Downie and
Michael Harris), and subsequent legislation on paper taxation
up to its abolition in 1850, as well as outlining controls by the
trade itself on pricing and the war over free trade in books in the
nineteenth century culminating in the Net Book Agreement of 1899.
To our sorrow, personal as well as bibliographical, he died some
three weeks before our meeting on 29 October, aged seventy-four.
Alan Downie was kind enough to step into the breach, but,
necessarily, with a slightly different paper which did not explain
our terminal dates. For this reason we have changed the title of

the conference papers. The plan, however, remains the same in broad outline: developments in various aspects of the book trade, including legislation, covered by Alan Downie's paper, periodical publishing, dealt with by Michael Harris, author-publisher relations with Mr Sutherland and Mr Thorogood, and the chronicling of these developments in Robin Myers's paper on John Nichols. There was also a sixth contribution which could not be included; this was an illustrated talk by James Mosley, Librarian of the St. Bride Printing Library, on 'William Caslon and the rise of English letter founding'.

Our thanks also go to all those who attended the conference and provided such a brisk commentary on the papers. Neither their discussion, nor the relaxed and friendly atmosphere in which it took place, allowing both established book trade scholars and librarians and novices to have their say, can be reproduced in our publication. It added much and we look forward to seeing many of those listed overleaf at our next conference.

Michael Harris and Robin Myers

London, February 1981

Notes on Contributors

Dr J.A. Downie is Lecturer in English Literature at Goldsmith's College, University of London. He is author of <u>Robert Harley and the Press</u>, Cambridge, 1979.

Dr Michael Harris has contributed articles and essays on the eighteenth-century newspaper press to several bibliographical publications and is currently joint editor of <u>The Newspaper in English Society</u> to be published later this year. He works for the University of London Extra-Mural Department.

Miss Robin Myers is Archivist of the Worshipful Company of Stationers, and is author of various bibliographical publications including <u>The British Book Trade from Caxton to the Present Day</u>, London, 1973.

Mr John Sutherland is Reader in English at University College, London, and is author of <u>Thackeray at Work</u>, London, 1974; <u>Victorian Novelists and Publishers</u>, London, 1976 and <u>Best Sellers; Popular Fiction in the 1970s</u>, London, 1981.

Mr Peter Thorogood is Senior Lecturer at the Polytechnic of Central London, an authority on Thomas Hood, and author of 'Thomas Hood and the Progress of Cant', in <u>Papers in Research and Criticism</u>, London, 1978.

Conference Members

Miss J Bell

Miss S B Bindman

Julian Bingley, Esq.   Antiquarian Book Monthly Review
Publications Limited

Miss G Brett

A P Burton, Esq.   Museum Officer

John Chidley, Esq.   Messrs. Henry Sotheran Ltd.

S G Colverson, Esq.   Oxford Polytechnic Publishing Course

A S Cook, Esq.   India Office Library and Records

Miss A Creed   Bookseller

M J Crump, Esq.   Eighteenth-century Short-Title Catalogue,
The British Library

Miss A Day

Miss C Ferdinand   Eighteenth-century Short-Title Catalogue,
The British Library

Miss S Green

Dr B A Goldgar   Lawrence University, Wisconsin, U.S.A.

C M Hartley, Esq.   Librarian

Dr D Hawes   Polytechnic of Central London

J Hewish, Esq.   British Library

A W Huish, Esq.   Librarian

Miss M Hunt   North London Collegiate School

Dr Elizabeth James   British Library

Dr M J Jannetta   British Library

P A L Jones   The National Library of Wales

R D Kirkman, Esq.   Messrs. Henry Sotheran Ltd.

Mrs L Knowles	
Mrs H A Lawrence	Librarian
Mrs B Lee	
Miss H Long	Melbourne, Australia
Dr G S Lumsden	
I Maxted, Esq.	Librarian
Mrs C Morris	Bookseller
Ms M Morris	
J A Owston, Esq.	Librarian
M R Perkin, Esq.	Liverpool University Library
Mrs E Potter	
K F Price, Esq.	Librarian
Miss C Purcell	
Miss E Rees	National Library of Wales
Miss D Rodger	Institute of Latin American Studies
D Ruane Wallis	
Mrs P Ruane Wallis	
R J S Shaw, Esq.	University of London
Miss J Small	Bookseller
J Sprague, Esq.	Messrs. Henry Sotheran Ltd.
P Stevenson, Esq.	
Mrs M Stevenson	
P Stockham, Esq.	Bookseller
Mrs D K Taylor	Queen Mary College Library
J Thorp, Esq.	Bookseller
Professor M Treadwell	Trent University, Canada
D Trudell, Esq.	

John Nichols (1745-1826), Chronicler of the Book Trade

Robin Myers

'Mr. Nichols', the Oxford printer Daniel Prince[1] told the antiquary
Richard Gough[2] - and Nichols recorded it in the Literary Anecdotes[3] -
'is one of those laborious and truly useful Gentlemen who do not spare
pains to preserve and inform Posterity in Literary History...' As
a publisher, a printer, an editor, an antiquary, he moved in many
worlds. Everywhere he garnered materials for biographical and
historical research, producing 'a mine of rough materials', as he
put it in the Advertisement to the Bibliotheca Topographica, 1796,
'whence a fair superstructure can be raised'. The Literary Anecdotes
and similar volumes of reminiscences were reckoned by Samuel Leigh
Sotheby (in his quaintly titled Ramblings in the Elucidation of the
Autograph of Milton, 1861) to be 'the storehouses of information of
past centuries. While they delight and feed the imagination, they
sow seeds of a succession of intellectual harvests. ' 'He never affected
to possess any superior share of erudition or to be profoundly versed
in the learned languaged', he wrote of himself, 'content, if in plain
and intelligible terms, in conversation or writing, he could contribute his quota of information or entertainment. '[4] For nearly sixty-
five years, he had a finger in almost every pie of literary, antiquarian or book trade concoction, from the age of thirteen, when he

was apprenticed to William Bowyer the Younger,[5] until his death
at the advanced age (by the standards of the day, very) of nearly
eighty. He made it his business to know all the gossip of an incredibl
gossipy, inbred society, and it was his business, his living, to recor
it.

His master, later business partner and benefactor, William
Bowyer, laid the foundation of Nichols's book trade career in many
ways. 'Wanted, apprentice, with some share of learning, the more
the better',[6] Bowyer would advertise. 'For more than half a century',
his protégé wrote in his Memoir of his master, 'he stood unrivalled
as a learned printer...' He was a man of high standards, of 'inflex-
ible probity' and a kind heart, with 'an uncommon alacrity in assisting the necessitous'.[7] But at the same time he was 'naturally fond
of retirement, he seldom went into company, unless with men of
letters; yet few perhaps, ever discriminated more justly the real
character of mankind... Too conscious, perhaps, of literary super-
iority he, in some instances, disgusted those best patrons of it - the
booksellers.'[8] He lived in an age that was beginning to allow a man
to go outside the sphere he was born into, but did not make him very
comfortable in his adopted one. He moved uneasily, though with
authority, in the separate worlds of trade and gentlemanly culture -
he rose to be Master of the Stationers' Company as well as being a
Fellow of the recently founded Society of Antiquaries, to whose
Archaeologia he contributed several papers. Nichols followed him
in both honours. Bowyer was a sensitive man, fairly easily huffed;
'it was a peculiarity, if it might be so called', explained Nichols,

in the character of Mr. Bowyer that his engagements as
a man of business never were sufficient to divest him of
those sensibilities, which men conscious of their super-
iority in respect of literary abilities sometimes experience to be not among the blessings of a learned education.
As he knew himself the first in this profession, he dis-
dained the servility of solicitation; but, when he saw
himself neglected, or another preferred where friendship
gave him a claim, he did not suppress the impulse of
resentment, which he felt on such occasions...

Speaking of Cambridge he said, 'My Father, (good man!) sent me
thither to qualify me by a new kind of experiment, for a printer, but
it served only in trade to expose me to more affronts, and to give
me a keener sensibility to them...'[9] As the son of a printer, and
grandson of a grocer, his standing in the commercial world was high,
but among gentry he would be below the salt. He lived (as which of us
ever did not?) in an age of transition, when scholarship began to ignore
social bounds. The hold, though not the prestige, of the Stationers'
Company over the book trade was waning, and power within the Company
was shifting from the printers to the booksellers. Bowyer, trained as
a printer, became a bookseller as well, and made an increasingly
lucrative thing by selling his own 'copies', preferably wholesale.
Nichols, unlike his proud, shy master, 'had none of the irascible
passions',[10] Chalmers[11] wrote of him, which may have endeared him
to one so conscious of snobberies and slights. Nichols was slow to
take offence, although he would not have his bona fides questioned.
Among the letters in the Bodleian not printed in the Anecdotes is one
to the Reverend Thomas Nash, whose book he printed. He was clearly
a difficult and suspicious author to whom Gough, as Nichols's editor,
wrote: 'To go on under such severe imputations is more than becomes
me to bear.'[12]

Usually, however, he remained equable, even when, in later
years he lost printing contracts for the learned societies, to Bulmer
and Bensley.[14] When Sir Joseph Banks[15] wrote to explain that 'the on
reason for the Change' of the printer for the Royal Society's publications was 'a preference to the new modes of Printing which no-one
but Mr. Bulmer can execute', Nichols printed the letter in the
Illustrations[16] and gave a description of 'Fine Printing' which
manages (just) to avoid the snide. The portrait of him that we
reproduce as our Frontispiece looks genial enough to me but Dibdin
asked of it: 'What have we here? The very septuagenarian himself. -
with his "rectangular cane"...about to give a rap upon the peri-
cranium of the saucy Zoilus who dares to question the loveliness of
the forms of his puncheons. '[17] He was flattered by the honours that
came to him in his sixties; to be Master of the Stationers' Company
in 1804 was to realise 'the summit of his ambition' and although he
had lost the printing of the Antiquaries in 1798, he was pleased to be
elected Fellow (1810) for his magnum opus, the History of Leicester
shire, 7 vols., 1795-1811. It is a work, by the by, where you can
find quite a crop of book trade material on anyone with Leicestershir
connections.

But he was too bland for some; his encomiums, which make
everyone someone until no-one is anyone, were criticised by Horace
Walpole, who could be much more scathing. Of the 1782 Biographica
and Literary Anecdotes of Bowyer he wrote, 'I wish it deserved the
pains he has bestowed on it every way, and that he would not dub so
many men great. I have known several of his heroes, who were very
little men. ' At the same time Walpole conceded that 'he scarce ever

saw a book so correct'. Perhaps Nichols was a bit obsequious, but still plain good nature shines from that homely, full-moon countenance emphasised by round glasses that do nothing for his looks, above a figure that was 'short and inclined to fulness'.

Not only was he the model of the good apprentice in being good-tempered, eager and grateful, but 'From his youth', Chalmers wrote, 'he did everything quickly, he read with rapidity...he spoke quickly, and that whether in the reciprocity of conversation, or when, which was frequently the case, he had to address the company in a set speech. He had also accustomed himself to write with great rapidity; but this, he used jocularly to allow, although a saving of time, did not tend to improve his hand.'[18] 'He possessed', Chalmers wrote on another page, 'not only extraordinary judgement in the allotment of his hours but equally extraordinary health and spirits to sustain him amidst the intenseness of industry and the frequent calls of complicated avocations.'[19]

Nichols learnt much more than the techniques of his craft from Bowyer, who inculcated a love of the history of the Trade in his receptive pupil, which they explored together to the very end of Bowyer's life.

After Bowyer's first stroke Nichols wrote to William Tooke,[20] his former fellow apprentice, 10 December 1774, one who also had 'some share of learning', leaving the Trade to become an historian of Russia and one of the editors of the General Biographical Dictionary; 'Since his last illness he has turned his thoughts to the Art of Printing, and we have been all this week, I mean he and I as an Amanuensis immersed in Mattaire, Middleton,[21] Palmer[22] and Meerman,[23] we

have plenty of materials. I wish you were here to compile and to
correct them as Mr. Bowyer, I fear will not have the strength to
go through with it, or I sufficient leisure to attend to it. '[24] But,
before the year was out he was writing to Tooke, 'I have written
a book...which must speak for itself; you will see it is an hasty
production... such as it is, however, let me persuade you to set
to work upon it at your leisure, and we may be able at some
future time to make an useful publication between us. The subject is the Origin of Printing. '[25] Nichols is referring to a reprint
of Conyers Middleton's Dissertation Concerning the Origin of
Printing in England (first ed. 1735 with a translation from the
Dutch of Baron Gerard Meerman's Origines Typographicae, 1767).
Nichols explained in the Anecdotes of Bowyer that 'the original
idea of this little pamphlet was Mr. Bowyer's; the completion of
it, his partner's'.[26]

   There was very little formal book trade history in England befor
the eighteenth century and most of it was concerned with the beginnings of printing. There are snippets of book trade history to be
found in biographical and topographical surveys such as Leland's
Itinerary, 1549,[27] known to the eighteenth century in Hearne's
editions of 1710-12 etc.; John Bale's Index Britanniae Scriptorum[28]
was known through Fuller's Worthies[29] (posthumously published
1662 etc.) which translates Bale's description of Caxton as 'a man
by no means dull nor benumbed by sloth' ('vir non omnino stupidus,
aut ignavi torpens', says Bale). It is an epithet that might apply to
Nichols himself. Fuller's annotated copy of the Worthies passed
into the hands of William Oldys,[30] contributor to the Biographia

Britannica and editor of The British Librarian (1737). As far as I
know the first English work that purports to be entirely about
printing history, unmixed with biography or topography, is Richard
Atkyns's The Original and Growth of Printing, 1664: purports, I
say, because it was in fact a missile in the pamphlet war against
the power of the Stationers' Company. Atkyns invented a manuscript
in Lambeth Palace Library and fabricated the story of a Dutch
printer, one Frederick Corsellis, whom Caxton helped to smuggle
into England to print the first English-printed book in Oxford, a
Rufinus commentary misdated 1468 for, as we now know, 1478.
Caxton, by this preposterous yarn, thus ceased to be England's
proto-typographer. If you could believe that you could believe anything, but the 'Corsellis myth' was perpetuated in an erratic work,
'very inaccurate even for the time in which it was written', say
Bigmore and Wyman; Samuel Palmer's General History of Printing,
1732, is the first complete history of English printing so it is a
pity that it is a thoroughly bad book. George Psalmanazar,[31] the
'false Formosan', maintained that he ghosted it for Palmer and in
the Literary Anecdotes, Nichols reprinted the account in Psalmanazar's
Auto-biography, (published posthumously) of how he came to take
the job on.[32] There is no hint that Nichols does not think Psalmanazar
perfectly trustworthy and knowledgeable. How much was written by
Psalmanazar may not be known, but it may be significant that it was
published in the year of Psalmanazar's death.

    Conyers Middleton's monograph skilfully demolished the 'Corsellis
myth' in an attempt to undo the harm done by Palmer's perpetuation
of it. His Essay is a landmark in incunable scholarship. After having

made an exhaustive search for the missing Lambeth manuscript,
he examined critically the evidence for its ever having existed,
and he considered that it might perhaps have been forged by Atkyns
himself. He also examined Caxton's types and compared them with
those used in the Rufinus commentary. His view was maintained in
the first biography of Caxton; John Lewis,[33] vicar of Margate,
produced a life of 'Mayster Wyllyam Caxton' two years after
Conyers Middleton, which despite inaccuracies and archaic spelling
in the title, has the merit of perspicacity, and of recognising the
importance of Middleton's findings. It might be supposed that that
would be the end of the matter, but Meerman revived the Corsellis
myth in his Origines Typographicae if only with the patriotic motive
of proving that Coster, not Gutenberg, was Europe's first printer.
In an appended exchange of letters between Meerman and Dr Ducarel,
Keeper of Lambeth Library, Meerman stood firm against scholarly
reasoning, with very weak arguments.

Bowyer and Nichols explained in the preface of their edition that
'the present publication had been first designed to have been extended
no farther than to reprint the substance of Dr. Middleton's Dissertation...' Then they decided to publish the companion monograph.
Nichols could never leave well alone so he added 'remarks thrown
into the form of Notes on Some Mistakes of that ingenious Gentleman'
which he put at the foot of the pages of Middleton's monograph. These
do credit to Nichols's assiduity but not to his critical acumen. In 1794,
Ralph Willett, the antiquary,[35] contributed to Archaeologia a 'memoi
on the origin of printing'; 'After what had been written by Dr. Ducare
and Dr. Middleton concerning the Lambeth MSS', he wrote,

I little expected that the subject would have been revived
by such respectable writers as Mr [sic] Meerman, and
Messrs Bowyer and Nichols; the latter, indeed, little
more than transcribe the sentiments of the former;
however, as they possess a considerable rank in literature, and explain and strengthen as far as they are
able, the arguments of the other writers they are well
entitled to the observations I shall attempt to make on
what they have written.[36]

In short, Nichols (for the notes were his, and signed with his
initials) had made a fool of himself but he gives the references to
the Archaeologia article in his long note on Willett and his library,
in the 'Annals' of 1776.[37] Keith Maslen, the Bowyer scholar, is
inclined to think that Nichols could not believe that book trade
history could be of general interest to his readers, or worth sub-
jection to scholarly method. It may be significant that there is
only a passing mention of the edition of the Dissertations in the
life of Middleton in the Literary Anecdotes,[38] where Nichols con-
centrates on the theological writings.

Meanwhile Lewis was trying to persuade Joseph Ames,[39]
book collector and first Secretary of the Antiquaries, to write a
general history of printing, with the aid of his own notes and
papers relating to his biography of Caxton. But Ames, knowing
of Palmer's forthcoming work 'at first felt unequal to an under-
taking of so great an extent', Nichols explained in his life of Ames,[40]
'But when Mr. Palmer's book came out, it by no means answered
the expectations of Mr. Lewis or Mr. Ames, or those of the public in general.' No Nicholean comment on why not. 'Mr. Ames...
at length consented to apply himself to the task; and after 25 years
spent in collecting and arranging his materials...published in one

volume 1749, his <u>Typographical Antiquities.</u>' Ames understood the
requirements of the job, and for this reason, 'I do ingenuously
confess', he wrote diffidently in his preface, 'that...I have undertaken a task much too great for my abilities, the extent of which
I did not so well perceive at first...' The fact is that Ames's
work though seminal, contains the first systematic identification
of the early English printers and the output of their presses. He
formulated, in a tentative way, a method for the dating of undated
early books which, a century later, William Blades and Henry
Bradshaw built upon and developed into a system that has been used
ever since.

Ames died the year his book came out (1749) and his annotated
copy of the <u>Antiquities</u> came into the hands of William Herbert,[41]
a man of many worlds, a traveller in India, a print seller on old
London Bridge, and an antiquary (that ubiquitous eighteenth-century
occupation for gentlemen). Another twenty-five years passed while
Herbert collected his material for a revised and enlarged Ames's
work (1785-90) in three volumes. 'I might have continued this
beyond the terms which Mr. Ames assigned to himself', Herbert
wrote in his preface to the third volume, 'and thus might have
handed down to distant posterity the improvement of my contemporaries in this noble art. But the history of the mechanical part
has been fully handled by Mr. Mores[42] in his <u>History of Letter-
Founders</u>. Mr. Nichols has supplied anecdotes of literature at
large for the last half century, in his <u>Memoirs of Mr. Bowyer,</u>
the last of our learned printers.' (Many, by the by, from Caxton
to William Blades and including Nichols himself, in his older days,

despite his opinion of himself, have been dubbed 'learned printers'.)
The formal self-deprecation of Herbert's words carry a hint of an
awakening awareness of the different kinds of bibliographical study;
the work of Ames, Herbert and Conyers Middleton exemplified the
physical description of books and specific copies of books which
leads on to analytical and descriptive bibliography. Most of
Nichols's contribution is biographical and anecdotal, chiefly concerned with trade and personal relations; he shows the way to
historical bibliography. Mores's work leads to the history and
close study of letter-forms.

Edward Rowe Mores was an antiquary of an unusual turn for his
century; he had an interest in type and the casting of type and he
'devoted many of the later years of this life', wrote William Blades,
'to the collection of old moulds and matrices. He purchased the
whole stock of the last of the old race of letter-founders, Mr. James
of Bartholomew Close, whose extensive collection was said to date
from the days of Wynken de Worde; and it is much to be regretted
that, after the death of Mr. Mores, his collections were not pre-
served intact.'[43] The sale of his effects in 1778 included a 'small
unpublished edition' (80 printed copies) of a 'very curious pamphlet'.
This was A Dissertation upon English Typographical Founders and
Founderies which Nichols bought up and, in his words, 'it was
given to the public in 1779, with the addition of a short explanatory
"appendix".'[44] Albert Smith observed that 'Nichols was certainly
aware of the dangers of introducing eccentricities into printing
practice just as he was alive to the importance of innovations, as
his appendix to Mores...shews.'[45] In 1783 he had proved himself

a talented type designer in designing the types for reproducing the Domesday Book, which was one of the Bowyer Press's finest productions; the types were cut by Joseph Jackson,[46] an apprentice to Caslon I. Nichols made use of Mores's Dissertation, true to his authorial and publishing form, in his Caslon entries in the Literary Anecdotes; he repeated Mores's account of the dispute between Caslon and Samuel Palmer, in which the former was befriended by the elder Bowyer. Publication of both the Typographical Founders and, two years later, the Memoirs of William Ged, 1781,[47] who introduced stereotyping into the British Isles, shows Nichols's interest in technical innovations in the early years of his maturity. Blades found Mores's account of the types used by Caxton and Wynken de Worde to be 'full of errors'. Nichols may have been unaware of this, but he recognised the importance of the Dissertation as a pioneer study of founders and letter forms and he put posterity in his debt once again by saving the book from the fate of Mores's collections of types. Much of Mores's work formed the basis of Talbot Baines Reed's History of Old English Letter Founders, 1887.

When William Herbert died (1795) his copy of the Typographical Antiquities, interleaved and bound in six volumes (now in the British Library), passed into the hands of that airy worshipper of Black Letter, Thomas Frognall Dibdin.[48] He projected a much more ambitious affair but only achieved one more volume – and an acknowledgement to Nichols.

The view of book trade history in England, then, was pretty limited when Nichols took the field with his joint edition of The Origin of Printing. Bowyer died in 1777 leaving to Nichols a very

prosperous business with a history to it, and ledgers back to 1699
intact.

1778 was, for Nichols, the annus mirabilis: he became co-editor
of the Gentleman's Magazine with David Henry, [49] brother-in-law
of its founder, Edward Cave[50]. This changed everything for
Nichols and turned him into a master chronicler of the Trade and
the literary world of his time. Henry was primarily a printer, but
in 1781 Nichols's firm took over the printing. Then, from 1782
until his death in 1826, Nichols was sole editor as well. Shortly
before his death Henry, feeling his eighty-two years, wrote to
Nichols; 'Finding myself unfit for the Business of the Magazine
and sensible how much I trespass on your Time and Patience in
supplying my Defects, I beg leave to submit the whole and entire
management of it with the Salary annexed into your Hands, in sure
and certain hope of seeing it flourish in greater Perfection from
the Improvement it will receive from an able Compiler.'[51] And it
did. The period of Nichols's influence, commented Edward Hart,
in Minor Lives, 1971, 'extended over 48 years, and during this
time the Gentleman's Magazine remained at the height of its influence'. Nichols, the man of many schemes and many contacts
made all roads lead to the Gentleman's Magazine. It provided the
material for those other schemes which, in turn, supplied material
for the Magazine. For thirty-four years, as Sylvanus Urban III,
Nichols was the Magazine's proprietor, editor and printer as well
as being author of large chunks of it. From the time of taking
over joint editorship, 'not a single month has elapsed', Nichols
wrote in his third person substitute for the journalistic 'we',[52]

'in which he has not written several articles in that miscellany;
some of them with his name or his initials and others (as is
essential in a periodical work) anonymously under the signatures,
very frequently either of Alphonso, Eugenio, M. Green, a London
Antiquary, etc. ' Of him it might be said, as Dr Johnson said of
Edward Cave, 'He never looked out of his window but with a view
to the Gentleman's Magazine. ' Nichols conducted the Magazine as
a combination of reference periodical and of magazine in the
modern sense. He greatly enhanced its usefulness as a reference
tool, especially for later ages, by commissioning Samuel
Ayscough[53] to compile an index to the first fifty-six volumes
(1786) and in 1819 two more were added for the intervening
years. To this, Nichols characteristically prefaced a history of
the Magazine. As soon as he took over as editor with David
Henry in 1782, he started to build up two sections particularly -
obituary notices (there was nothing like them until those of The
Times became a biographical source) and 'letters to the editor',
some of the latter written by Nichols himself under one of his
pseudonyms. As Edward Hart observes; 'Today the bound volumes
of the Gentleman's Magazine on the open shelves of the British
Library are among the most frequently consulted books in the
Library. ' Peter Pindar,[54] politically the antithesis of John
Nichols, lampooned the Nichols fact-finding industry, all grist
to the obituary mills, in a half-crown pamphlet printed by
Kearsley: A Benevolent Epistle to Sylvanus Urban, alias Master
John Nichols, 1790:

> Poor souls! The dying dread thee more than death.
> 'Oh save us from John Nichols! is the cry
> Let not that death-hunter know where we lie;
> What in delirium from our lips may fall,
> Oh! hide—our letters, burn them all...

He pictures Nichols's quarry as

> Condemned alas, to grin with grisly mien,
> 'midst the pale horrors of his Magazine.

1778 was also the year that Nichols published his 'little brochure' of fifty-two pages in twenty copies of Biographical Memoirs of William Bowyer, undertaken as a homage, ex voto optimi, amicissimi. Albert Smith suggests that Nichols's practice of printing pamphlets for private circulation, was done 'chiefly with the idea of stimulating the recipients to contribute further information'. A few printed copies didn't cost a printer much, less than typed copies would now. A slightly shortened version of the Memoirs, complete with footnotes, was reprinted in the Gentleman's Magazine.[55] This, explains Edward Hart, 'set the pattern, both for the gradual enlargement and for the interdependence of the Anecdotes and the Gentleman's Magazine'. The quarto, The Biographical and Literary Anecdotes, 1782, had more footnotes and by the time Nichols arrived at the fullest version, The Literary Anecdotes of the Eighteenth Century, the footnotes were longer yet, and there were footnotes to footnotes, and addenda to boot - the main text sometimes being pushed quite off the page. The first three of the nine-volume Literary Anecdotes comprise 'Annals of Mr. Bowyer's press'. The latter volumes go off on biographical and bibliographical areas unconnected with Bowyer but they still have Bowyeriana scattered throughout.

Nichols's memory stretched vicariously back 100 years before his own time, for the Elder Bowyer had been apprentice to Miles Flesher,[56] grandson of Miles Flesher, Master of the Stationers' Company. By drawing on the Bowyer ledgers and files of correspondence, and by conversing with fellow printers, booksellers and customers of the Bowyer Press, Nichols was able to supply much accurate information about firms the Bowyers dealt with in the latter half of the seventeenth and early eighteenth centuries, all of which would otherwise have been lost to succeeding generations.

Before Nichols, what there was of book history was directed to the fifteenth-century beginnings of English printing, where Nichols was weakest; he was strongest in the areas, now of such bibliographical interest, of the sixteenth to eighteenth centuries.

Serendipity is all very well for a bedside book, but a reference work needs a good index to 'assist the Forgetful and direct the Inquisitive' (volume vii of the Literary Anecdotes transforms a rambling work into an effective aid to research. 'For not to be able to find what we know is in our possession, is a more vexatious circumstance than the mere want of what we have neglected to procure. '[57]). Nichols commissioned the index volume from his nephew - Samuel Bentley,[58] elder brother of the publisher Richard Bentley, a printer and antiquary like his uncle, and a partner in the firm (1812-18).

Book and newspaper publishing were not then the separate worlds they were later to become; hence the interdependence of the Literary Anecdotes and the Gentleman's Magazine. Newspaper history was one of Nichols's interests. Volume iv of the Literary

Anecdotes contains sixty-four pages 'Of publick news and weekly

papers; when they first began; their progress, increase, and uses

and abuses to the people'. There is a sixty-page list of papers

based on the Harleian Manuscript list which was

> so extremely incomplete, that I had taken some con-
> siderable trouble to improve it, from the entries at
> Stationers' Hall, and from the Royal Collection in the
> British Museum, before I was aware that Mr Chalmers
> had encountered a similar labour. This, however, is
> very far from superseding the list here given; which,
> by the kind co-operation of my friend the Rev. Samuel
> Ayscough... contains a considerable number which
> escaped the notice of Mr Chalmers; and, being continued
> to a later period from a valuable collection of newspapers
> in my own possession, may now be considered as tolerably
> complete. '

This collection is now in the Bodleian. [59] Wilkes also gave Nichols

a collection of thirty-five folio volumes of newspapers collected

between 1768 and 1779, 'illustrated with many manuscript remarks

by himself, detached printed papers on various subjects, and some

curious caricatures'. But these were filched by a rascally servant

and'never afterwards could be traced, having probably been con-

signed, as waste paper, to the shop of some distant cheesemonger'.

Nichols also reprinted Oldys's article on the related subject of

'the origin of pamphlets'. [60]

Between publication of the Biographical Anecdotes and the

extensive revision, Nichols's business premises in Red Lion

Passage was gutted by fire, 8 February 1808, just four weeks

after he had fallen and fractured his thigh. He considered a broken

femur a mere nothing compared with the 'far greater calamity of the destruction of his printing office and warehouses, with the whole of their valuable contents', as he described it in the Gentleman's Magazine the following week. The loss included his annotated copy of the Literary Anecdotes which had been printed off in 1802 ready for subsequent publication. The fire delayed publication for a further four years but 'he had the resolution to apply with redoubled diligence to literary and typographical labours'.[61] He had intended to retire three years later, but in the event he more or less died in harness. He was well insured, and the Trade rallied round, as they had in the case of the elder Bowyer's fire, and it seems as though his material prosperity was the least of it. No sooner was the last volume of the Literary Anecdotes off the stocks than Nichols set to work on the sequel, Illustrations of the Literary History of the Eighteenth Century. With the help of his son John Bowyer Nichols, who had been taken into partnership in 1801, he published four volumes, 1817-22?, and John Bowyer completed a further four volumes (to 1858) after his father's death, concluding with an index and a memoir of his father by Alexander Chalmers, editor and biographer, son of a printer and one of the later editors of the General Biographical Dictionary. The Illustrations are not up to the standard of the Literary Anecdotes because they are over-full of letters, and the editorial comment is sparse and often dull; the work lacks the sparkle and the personal touch of the first series; there is, too, a gradual falling off as the volumes progress; the original inspiration of their creator was lost as the people and events receded in the memory. But that is not to

say that the Illustrations are not marvellously and irreplaceably
useful for researchers into the nineteenth century.

Nichols included a number of substantial articles on general
aspects of the Trade in the Literary Anecdotes. A 'History of the
Stationers' Company', followed by a list of its benefactors helped
to fill up volume iii (Nichols liked to print off in even workings,
long ahead of publication). His history of the Company is the first
and only straightforward account we have, apart from a few nineteenth-century domestic pamphlets, until Cyprian Blagden's
definitive History of the Stationers' Company 1403-1959, 1960.
Volume iii is completed by Richard Gough's article on 'The
progress of selling books by catalogue' which looks forward to
Pollard and Ehrmann's Distribution of Books by Catalogue and
A.N.L. Mumby's writings in the same field. There is book trade
data, mainly biographical, scattered through much of Nichols's
other published work - the Select Poems, with Notes Biographical
and Historical, 8 vols., 1780-1811, the History of Leicestershire,
which effectively earned him election to the Society of Antiquaries,
and the Bibliotheca Topographica which Nichols and Gough edited
jointly in fifty-two numbers, 1780-90, and then re-issued in nine
volumes, 1812-15.

In the small, almost claustrophobic, world which Nichols moved
in, there was a good deal of taking in of others' intellectual washing,
of exchange of information, and of mutual acknowledgement. The
second, scholarly edition of Oldys's Biographia Britannica, 1778-95,
has evidence that the editor, Andrew Kippis[62] and Nichols pooled
some data; Kippis was a contributor to the Gentleman's Magazine;

Dibdin's Bibliographical Decameron draws heavily on the Literary
Anecdotes (with acknowledgement) particularly for the third
volume, 'the ninth day'; while Nichols includes Dibdin in his
acknowledgements. Edward Hart points out that the Gentleman's
Magazine and the Literary Anecdotes are a source for Isaac
D'Israeli's[63] pioneer studies of authorship, the Calamities of
Authors, 1813, and the Quarrels of Authors, 1814. Nichols
acknowledged D'Israeli's help and listed him among the contributors to volume viii of the Literary Anecdotes which came out
the same year as the Quarrels of Authors. Both were reviewed
in the Gentleman's Magazine, the former in June, the latter in
September 1814. Hart finds:

> specific evidence that Nichols and D'Israeli assisted
> each other in delving into the relationship between Pope
> and Lintot. [64]D'Israeli, for example, uses some of
> Nichols's own phrasing, from volume viii, and D'Israeli's
> book was published several months before Nichols's,
> indicating that D'Israeli had access to Nichols's Manuscript
> or to certain printed pages before they were published...
> This example of mutual assistance...illustrates the kind
> of relationship that existed between Nichols and nearly
> all other anecdotists and antiquaries of his day. [65]

D'Israeli wrote in his Preface: 'Of my old and respected friend
Mr John Nichols, who has devoted a life to Literature...it is no
common gratification for me to add, that he has...zealously aided
my researches.' Nichols was always equally scrupulous in his
acknowledgements. Edward Hart observed that 'in working closely
with him over a period of 20 years, I have yet to find an example
of his using another man's work without acknowledgement'. The
same cannot be said of those who came after him. Indeed, we all

plunder Nichols shamelessly, for his 'storehouse of information of past centuries'[66] is all there for the taking. Edward Hart points out that 'there is not a life of a literary figure of the 18th century included in the DNB that is not indebted to some extent to John Nichols... some continuing Nichols's original phraseology; in a few instances whole sentences are transplanted unaltered.' A list of some of his debtors is given in the appendix to this paper.

The Gentleman's Magazine continued its high standard throughout Nichols's lifetime, despite the fire. After he died, it started on a downward path until, in 1868, after a change of both printer and publisher, it became an entirely new publication with another character. Its last editor (1866-68) under the old régime was Edward Walford,[67] who tried, after the change, to keep up its biographical tradition with his Register and Magazine of Biography (1869 all published). Later he continued the Nicholsean tradition by editing the Antiquarian Magazine and Bibliographer (1881-6) under the imprint of Elliot Stock,[68] that bold and enterprising Victorian publisher of bibliography. Walford's relations with Stock were stormy in the extreme: 'the vile dragon of Paternoster Row' he called him in a letter to Andrew Tuer[69] in my possession.

Whatever the rights and wrongs of his business ethics we must be grateful to him for initiating several bibliographical and booklovers' series. One such was the retrospective Gentleman's Magazine Library, of thirty volumes under the general editorship of Laurence Gomme.[70] It was a 'classified collection of the chief contents of the Gentleman's Magazine from 1731-1869', brought out between 1883 and 1894. Two or three volumes collected book

articles, each bearing the date of first publication in the Magazine.
Literary Curiosities and Notes, 1888, subtitled 'facts in the history
of book-making' reprinted an 1852 article on the 'early use of
paper in England', and one signed 'Phosphorus' was the 1805
article on 'ink'. Bibliographical Notes, 1889, reissued 'the first
English newspaper established in England' in 1794. Nichols's
scattered contributions to book history were thus handily re-
assembled for Victorian delectation and the use of later generations
of bibliographers. Timperley's[71] Dictionary of Printers and
Printing, with the Progress of Literature, Ancient and Modern,
1839, is the poor man's substitute for the Literary Anecdotes and
the Illustrations, being all, or more than, meagre purses and
private book space can run to. The reissue, An Encyclopaedia of
Printing..., 1842, includes a manual of printing and, say Bigmore
and Wyman, 'meagre particulars of printers and booksellers from
1839 to 1842'. The Dictionary was produced 'to render some information on the subject attainable in as cheap a manner as possible...'
It is, however, not merely a cut-down 'Nichols', for the author
acknowledges himself indebted to the works of many British bibliographers, 'last, not least, to the pages of Mr Urban, for the
notices of modern printers and booksellers'.[72] A comparison of
specific entries in Nichols and Timperley shows that the
Dictionary is 'Nichols' with the stuffing out, or, as the infant
Edmund Gosse described a skeleton, 'a man with the meat off';
Charles Timperley was a working printer while John Nichols was
'Maecaenas to the learned'.

The odd thing is that John Nichols was not, it seems to me,

a man of genius; he was doing the fashionable thing, collecting
'ana', but he put posterity in his debt by printing letters and
comments whose originals have long since disappeared. Even so,
as Edward Hart points out, 'every year some of the lost letters
make an appearance in the Bodleian or the British Museum'.[73]
After the sale of the Gough correspondence in 1874, for example,
five of the eleven volumes then catalogued disappeared, but in
1975 the Bodleian bought a quantity of what I suppose was some
of the missing material at a sale at Sotheby's. Hart does not
mention it as his book predates that sale. Nichols's collecting
and publishing activities were of the same kind as those of his
contemporaries but they were greater in intensity because he was
a particularly energetic man and, as a prosperous bookseller,
editor and printer, he was in a position to publicise his work better
through the interlocking media of the Gentleman's Magazine and
the Literary Anecdotes; and he was at the centre of a dynasty of
anecdotists whose collective memory began with the elder Bowyer,
or even Miles Flesher the Younger in the seventeenth century,
and stretched as far forward as the death of his grandson, the
printer, publisher and antiquary John Gough Nichols (died 1873).

'If asked, why Printers and Booksellers in particular',
Timperley quotes Nichols on the title page of his Dictionary, 'I
answer, they are a valuable class of the community – the friendly
assistants, at least, if not the patrons of literature – and I myself
one of the fraternity...'

Notes

Abbreviations used:

LA   J. Nichols, Literary Anecdotes of the Eighteenth Century,
      9 vols., 1782-1815   •

IL   J. Nichols and J. B. Nichols, Illustrations of the Literary
      History of the Eighteenth Century, 8 vols., 1817-58

GM   Gentleman's Magazine

ALs   Autograph Letter signed

Hart E. L. Hart, Minor Lives, 1971

1. Daniel Prince, (d. 1796) Oxford printer and bookseller, one
   of the oldest booksellers in England, LA ii, iii, vi, viii;
   IL, iv, v; Bigmore and Wyman, Bibliography of Printing;
   Plomer, Dictionary of Printers; Timperley, Dictionary of
   Printing (see Appendix).

2. Richard Gough (1735-1809), Director of the Society of Antiquaries
   (1771), contributor to the GM as 'D. H. ', edited Camden, collaborated with Nichols, editor of Nichols's press. He and Nichols
   made excursions through England for twenty years. LA, i-vi,
   vii, ix; IL, iv, v, viii; but mainly LA, vi. 262-626.

3. LA, iii. 694.

4. LA, vi. 630; IL, viii, preface (p. vii).

5. William Bowyer, the Younger (1712-1777). LA, i. 2-420, viii;
   IL, ii-iv, vi.

6. LA, iii. 286n.

7. LA, iii. 269.

8. LA, iii. 270.

9.Ibid.

10.<u>IL</u>, viii, preface (p. xxxiv).

11.Alexander Chalmers (1759-1854), son of Scots printer.
Editor of the <u>Biographical Dictionary</u> (1812-17 edition),
wrote memoir of Nichols in <u>GM</u> and <u>IL</u>. <u>LA</u>, i, ii, v, viii,
ix; <u>IL</u>, iv-vi, viii.

12.Bodleian MSS Eng. Lett. b. 13.

13.William Bulmer (1767-1830), 'fine' printer, friend of Thomas
Bewick, printer to the Royal Society (1792-). <u>IL</u>, iv, vi.

14.Thomas Bensley (d. 1833), 'fine' printer, printed for the
Society of Antiquaries (1798-1821) at which point Nichols
got the contract back. <u>LA</u>. viii. 417.

15.Sir Joseph Banks (1743-1820), President of the Royal Society,
natural historian. <u>LA</u>, ii-iv, vi, viii, ix; <u>IL</u>, i, iii-viii.

16.<u>IL</u>, iv. 697.

17.T. F. Dibdin, <u>Bibliographical Decameron</u>, ii. 403 (see Appendix).
Dibdin uses an earlier portrait, but refers to the one we reproduce, the Frontispiece to <u>IL</u>, viii.

18.<u>IL</u>, viii, preface (p. xxiv); <u>GM</u>, xcvi, December 1826.

19.<u>IL</u>, viii, preface (p. xxxi); <u>GM</u>, xcvi.

20.William Tooke (1744-1820), apprenticed, with John Nichols, to
W. Bowyer, the Younger. Historian of Russia after travelling
there. Editor of <u>General Biographical Dictionary</u>, 1798, chaplain
(according to J. Lewis, <u>History of Islington</u>, 1840, p. 163n) to
the Stationer's Company. <u>LA</u>, i-iii, vi.

21.Conyers Middleton (1683-1750), theologian, classical scholar,
Fellow of Trinity College, Cambridge. Author of <u>Dissertation</u>

on the Origin of Printing, 1735 (see Appendix). LA, i–iii, v, vi, viii, ix; IL, i–v.

22. Samuel Palmer (d. 1732), printer in Bartholomew Close, employed Benjamin Franklin in his printing office. Nominal author of The General History of Printing, 1732 (see Appendix). LA, i, ii, iv, v, viii; IL, iv.

23. Baron Gerard Meerman (1722–1771), collector, whose collections formed the foundations of the Museum Meermanum, the Hague. Author of Origines Typographicae, 1767 (see Appendix). LA, ii, vi, viii; IL, iii, iv.

24. ALs to William Tooke, 10 December 1774 in Columbia University Nichols Collection.

25. Ibid.

26. LA, iii. 174.

27. John Leland (1506–52), first British antiquary, librarian and antiquary to Henry VIII before 1530. Author of Itinerary, 1710 and Collectanea, 1715. LA, i–vi, viii; IL, iv.

28. John Bale (1495–1563), religious dramatist, historian of English writers. IL, iv, v.

29. Thomas Fuller (1608–61), church historian of Britain, historian of Cambridge (1655). Author of The Worthies of England, 1662. LA, i, ii, vi, viii, ix; IL, iii–v.

30. William Oldys (1696–1761), herald and antiquary. Author of 'Dissertation on Pamphlets', The British Librarian, 1737, co-editor with Samuel Johnson, of the Harleian Miscellany, 1744–46, contributor to Biographia Britannica (1747–60), acquired Fuller annotated copy of The Worthies. LA, ii–vi, vii, ix; IL, iv, viii.

31.George Psalmanazar (1679?-1763), rascally impostor, self-styled Japanese Christian and Formosan etc. Contributor to The Universal History, 1750, Memoirs, 1764, ghosted Palmer's General History of Printing (see Appendix). LA, i-iii.

32.LA, ii.28.

33.John Lewis (1675-1747), vicar of Margate, first biographer of Caxton, Kent topographer, lent his Caxton notes to Ames. LA, i-iii, v, vi, ix; IL, iv, vi.

34.Andrew Coltee Duracel, F.S.A., F.R.S. (1713-85), born Normandy, antiquary, Keeper of Lambeth Palace Library (1757-). LA, i-vi, viii, ix; IL, iv, vi.

35.Ralph Willett, F.S.A., F.R.S. (1719-95), collector of early printed books, block books, prints and drawings.

36.Archaeologia, xi.154ff.

37.LA, iii.7n.

38.LA, iv.171 and 177.

39.Joseph Ames (1689-1759), bibliographer, antiquary, collector of early printed books, first Secretary of the Society of Antiquaries. LA, v, viii; IL, iii, iv, vi.

40.LA, v.258.

41.William Herbert (1718-95), bibliographer, worked and travelled in India (c. 1748). Print seller on London Bridge, did second edition of Atkyns's Gloucestershire and of Ames's Typographical Antiquities (see Appendix). LA, i-iii, v, viii, ix; IL, iv-vii.

42.Edward Rowe Mores (1731-78), antiquary, collections now in British Library and Bodleian. Author of Dissertation upon Typographical Founders (see Appendix). LA, i-iii, v, viii, ix; IL, iii-vi.

43. W. Blades, Biography and Typography of William Caxton, 1882, p.109.

44. LA, vi. 631.

45. See Appendix - 'Modern accounts and assessments of Nichols'.

46. Joseph Jackson (1733-92), letter-founder, apprenticed to elder Caslon, cut types in Hebrew, Persian and Bengali.

47. William Ged (1696-1761), Scots inventor of stereo typing, or at least introduced it into Britain. LA, ii, vi, viii.

48. Thomas Frognall Dibdin (1776-1847), 'bibliographer extra-ordinary'. LA, i, iii, vi, ix; IL, iv, vi, viii.

49. David Henry (1710-92), Scots brother-in-law of Edward Cave, printed second edition of GM, co-editor of GM with Nichols. LA, iii, v, vi, viii, ix.

50. Edward Cave (1691-1754), son of a Rugby cobbler, printer, 'furnished London news to country papers' etc. Founder of GM. LA, i, ii, v, viii, ix; IL, i, ii.

51. ALs from Henry to Nichols in Columbia University Nichols Collection.

52. LA, vi. 628.

53. Samuel Ayscough (1745-1804), indexer, booksellers' assistant, British Museum librarian, 'improved' Nichols's list of news-papers, indexed first 56 vols. of GM. LA, ii, iv, ix; IL, ii, iii, v.

54. John Wolcot alias Peter Pindar (1738-1819), political satirist and poet.

55. GM, September to December 1778, nos 409-12, 449-56, 513-16, 669-74.

56. Miles Flesher the Younger, grandson of the elder Miles Flesher,

the law patentee etc., generally confused with him. The young

Miles Flesher was the elder Bowyer's master. I am grateful

to Professor Michael Treadwell for disentangling the two

M. Fleshers for me. LA, i, iii.

57.GM, lcvi, index.

58.Samuel Bentley (1785-1868), printer, antiquary, brother of

Richard Bentley, publisher (1794-1871), partner of John Nichols

(1808-18), compiled index to LA, viii.

59.LA, iv; 'Of Public News and Weekly Papers', 37-8: Bodleian

Eng. Misc. c. 138.

60.LA, v. 464.

61.LA, vi. 629.

62.Andrew Kippis (1725-95), dissenting clergyman, biographer,

contributor to GM, Monthly Review, New Annual Register,

second ed. Biographia Britannica, 6 vols., 1778-95. LA, i-vi,

vii, ix; IL, iv-vii.

63.Isaac D'Israeli (1776-1848), historian of authorship (see Appendix),

father of Benjamin Disraeli. LA, i-v, vii, ix; IL, iii.

64.Bernard Lintot (1675-1736), bookseller, published Pope's Rape of

the Lock, translations of the Iliad and Odyssey etc. LA, i, ii, vi.

65.Hart, p. 228.

66.S. L. Sotheby, see p. 1.

67.Edward Walford (1823-97), man of letters, hack journalist,

compiler, last editor of the GM in its original form.

68.Elliot Stock (1838-1911), publisher of bibliography etc. S.

Pantazzi, The Book Collector, 1971, xx. I. 25-46.

69.Andrew Tuer (1838-1900), publisher as Field and Tuer, writer on Bartolozzi and on children's literature.

70. George Laurence Gomme (1853-?), journalist and hack scholar, editor of the Gentleman's Magazine Library.

71. Charles Timperley (1794-1846?), printer, writer on topography, published Songs of the Press, 1833 and Encyclopaedia of Printing, 1830 etc.

72. Timperley, Dictionary of Printing, 1839, v, preface.

73. Hart, p.193.

Appendix: A Select Short-title Genealogy of Book Trade Histories

1. Before Nichols

R. Atkyns, The Original and Growth of Printing, 1664.

S. Palmer (i.e. G. Psalmanazar), A General History of Printing, 1732.

C. Middleton, A Dissertation Concerning the Origin of Printing in England, 1735.

J. Lewis, The Life of Mayster Wyllyam Caxton, 1737.

W. Oldys, The British Librarian, 1737, second ed. A. Kippis, 1778-95.

J. Ames, Typographical Antiquities, 1749; revised, W. Herbert, 3 vols., 1785-90; revised, T.F. Dibdin, 4 vols., 1810-14.

R. Watt, Bibliotheca Britannica, 4 vols., 1819-24.

2. Contemporary with Nichols

E.R. Mores, Dissertation upon Old English Typographical Founders and Founderies, 1778.

W. Oldys, revised Kippis (see above).

J. Ames, revised Herbert (see above).

J. Boswell, The Life of Samuel Johnson, 2 vols., 1791.

I. D'Israeli, Calamities of Authors, 1813.

I. D'Israeli, Quarrels of Authors, 1814.

J. Ames, revised Dibdin (see above).

T.F. Dibdin, A Bibliographical Decameron, 3 vols., 1817.

R. Watt, Bibliotheca Britannica, 4 vols., 1819-24.

3. By John Nichols

Biographical Memoirs of William Bowyer, 1778 (pr. ptd. in twenty copies).

Biographical and Literary Anecdotes of William Bowyer, 4to, 1782.

Literary Anecdotes of the Eighteenth Century, 9 vols., 1812-15 [16]

Illustrations of the Literary History of the Eighteenth Century, 8 vo
  1817-58, (last 4 vols. by John Bowyer Nichols).

The Gentleman's Magazine, ed. J. Nichols (1778-1826) (contains
  much material also in Literary Anecdotes and Illustrations).

3a. Book trade Studies edited by Nichols

W. Bowyer and J. Nichols eds., The Origin of Printing in Two
  Essays, 1774; revised 1776; revised with supplement by J.
  . Nichols, 1781.

Biographical Anecdotes of William Hogarth, 1780 (pr. ptd. in
  twelve copies); second ed., 1782; third ed., 1785; fourth ed.,
  1810; fifth ed., 1817.

Biographical Memoirs of William Ged, 1781.

J.B. Nichols and J. Nichols eds., Life and Letters of John Dunton,

3b. Book trade Material to be found in:

Select Collection of Poems, with Notes Biographical and Historical,
  8 vols., 1780-1811.

History of Leicestershire, 8 vols., 1795-1815.

R. Gough and J. Nichols eds., Bibliotheca Topographica Britanica,
  52 numbers, 1780-90; 9 vols., 1812-15.

[Samuel Pegge] J. Nichols ed., Anonymiana, 1809.

4. After Nichols

C. Timperley, A Dictionary of Printing, 1839.

H.G. Bohn ed., An Encyclopaedia of Printing, 1842.

J. Britton, Auto-Biography, 2 vols., 1850.

J. Rees and J. Britton, Reminiscences of Literary London (1779-1853), 1896.

C. Knight, Shadows of Old Booksellers, 1865.

H. Curwen, A History of Booksellers, the Old and the New, 1873 (Chapter 1: 'Booksellers of Olden Times' owes much to J. Nichols).

G. L. Gomme ed., The Gentleman's Magazine Library, 17 vols. in 30 parts, 1883-1905 (3 vols. on book history).

W. Roberts, The Earlier History of Bookselling, 1889.

E. Marston, Sketches of Booksellers of Other Days, 1901.

E. Marston, Sketches of Some Booksellers of the Time of Dr. Johnson, 1902.

The Dictionary of National Biography, 64 vols., 1882-90 (eighteenth century entries owe much to Nichols).

T. B. Reed, A History of Old English Letter Foundries, 1887.

E. C. Bigmore and C. W. Wyman, A Bibliography of Printing, 3 vols., 1880-96.

F. A. Mumby, The Romance of Bookselling, 1910, revised as, Publishing and Bookselling, 1930.

H. R. Plomer, A Dictionary of Printers and Booksellers who were at Work in England, Scotland and Ireland, 1725-75, 1932.

5. Biographical studies of John Nichols

J. Nichols, 'Brief memoirs of the author of these volumes', LA, vi. 627-39 (includes list of fifty-six publications to 1811).

A. Chalmers, 'memoir of John Nichols', IL, viii, preface (pp. i-xxv).

A. Chalmers, 'letters of condolence', IL, viii, preface (pp. xxv-xlviii), first printed in the Gentleman's Magazine, December, 1828, xcvi, pp. 489-504 (with list of publications).

<u>IL</u>, viii. 566-69. Further list of publications bringing the total
number of publications to seventy-one, by John Bowyer Nichols

T. F. Dibdin, 'visit to an octogenerian', <u>IL</u>, viii.

G. A. Aitken, 'John Nichols', <u>Dictionary of National Biography</u>.

A. Dobson, 'a literary printer', <u>National Review</u>, 1913, lxi. 1086-

6. Modern accounts and assessments of John Nichols

[G. E. Dunstone], <u>At the sign of Cicero's Head. A short history
of the House of Nichols (1699-1939)</u>, 1939.

G. Pollard, 'Puritans and scholars. John Nichols and his descen-
dants', <u>TLS</u>, 9 December 1939, p. 724.

G. B. Schick, 'Kind hints to John Nichols, by Joseph Warton and
others', <u>Notes & Queries</u>, new ser. 3, 1956, pp. 76-8.

A. H. Smith, 'John Nichols, printer and publisher', <u>The Library</u>,
5. viii, 3 September 1963, pp. 169-90.

J. M. Kuist, introduction to Kraus reprint of <u>The Works of John
Nichols</u>, 1968.

E. L. Hart, <u>Minor Lives : a collection of biographies by John
Nichols</u>, annotated with an introduction on John Nichols and
the antiquarian and anecdotal movements of the late eighteenth
century, 1971.

J. M. Kuist, 'The Gentleman's Magazine in the Folger Library;
the history and significance of the Nichols family collection',
<u>Studies in Bibliography</u>, 1976, pp. 307-21.

7. Nichols Source Material (see Hart,xiii, 167-8, 193-4)

British Library:

includes letters from Dr Johnson to Nichols (1778-84) and from

Joseph Warton to Nichols.

Bodleian:

includes what was 6 (out of 11) vols. of Richard Gough corres-

pondence, acquired before 1916.

a much larger collection bought in 1975, much relating to the

fire at Nichols's works, 1808.

collection of 305 vols. of newspapers (1672-1737) made by

Nichols.

Harvard University Library:

Sixteen letters to and from Dr Johnson.

Columbia University Special Collections, New York:

1,064 items acquired by the Typographic Library & Museum of

the American Type Founders Company (see Hart, viii.168).

'Most of these papers, though by no means all, are private family

letters. For a scholar studying Nichols...it is indispensible...

because the business was a family business, and...because

Nichols as a private man is revealed in this collection in glimpses

that he did not allow to appear in the public view of himself in his

works.'(Hart, viii.168.)

Folger Shakespeare Library, Washington D.C.:

4,500 items of Gentleman's Magazine material in bound volumes,

annotated by the editors, and a mass of correspondence with con-

tributors to the GM - presumably all post-fire (1808).

The Growth of Government Tolerance of the Press to 1790

Alan Downie

One of the preconditions necessary for the development of the book trade in the eighteenth century was the decline in legal restrictions governing the printing and publication of reading material. In the last three years the picture given by Laurence Hanson[1] and Frederick Seaton Siebert[2] of the growth of government tolerance of the press has been redrawn in a number of ways. Raymond Astbury has added important new details to our knowledge of the events surrounding the expiry of the Licensing Act in 1695,[3] while David Foxon's Sandars Lectures (1978) on the Stamp Act and my own, largely independent, political view of the introduction of the tax[4] have, I believe, raised fundamental questions about this crucial new law. This paper is an attempt to provide an overview of the rise of a free press in England in the light of recent findings. The circumstances through which this came about were primarily political in character. This, then, is predominantly a political overview.

In his Life of Samuel Johnson, James Boswell remarked, almost incredulously, upon the necessity of remaining anonymous as a reporter of parliamentary debates in the era of Walpole:[5]

Parliament then kept the press in a kind of mysterious
awe, which made it necessary to have recourse to such
devices. In our time it has required an unrestrained
freedom, so that the people in all parts of the kingdom
have a fair, open, and exact report of the actual proceedings of their representatives and legislators, which
in our constitution is highly to be valued...

Boswell succeeds in expressing, albeit in eighteenth-century

terms, a fundamental twentieth-century belief, for few people in

England today would deny the desirability of a full knowledge of

the affairs of Parliament. The crucial steps along the road to

freedom of the press took place in the eighteenth century, or,

more strictly, in the one hundred years following the Glorious

Revolution of 1688. Boswell's cri de coeur marks the terminal

point of my paper. The dedication of the first edition of his Life

of Johnson was signed 20 April 1791; his biography was largely

ready for the press by 1790. In 1792 Fox's Libel Act empowered

a jury, instead of a judge, to determine the criminality of a libel.

This was an important point, for any dangerous opposition

pamphlet had previously been open to prosecution as seditious

libel, with the outcome of the case a virtual certainty, as judges

were, or could be, susceptible to government pressure. But

when all is said, Fox's Libel Act merely reinforced earlier

barriers against government control of the press. The major

victory had been the overcoming of pre-publication censorship.

In the growth of government tolerance of the press in England

two dates were vital - with hindsight, at any rate: 1695 and 1712.

In 1695 the so-called Licensing Act was allowed to lapse. Its

expiry effectively meant the end of pre-publication censorship.

To Macaulay, this almost insignificant event, in contemporary eyes, was of more importance than the signing of Magna Carta or the acceptance by William and Mary of the Bill of Rights six years earlier. But we should not set too much stock by the mere lapse of government control. At the outset, the expiry was a legal issue, not a blow for press freedom. The press may have enjoyed for a time a de facto liberty: it had not yet won the right. The passing of the Stamp Act in 1712 indicated that the licensing system of pre-publication censorship had been superseded by a policy which sought not to impose a rigid set of restrictions upon the press, but to exploit its tremendous popularity by taxing newspapers and publications of a political nature. Again, with the benefit of hindsight, we can recognise that this was the crucial change in government attitudes. The Stamp Act remained in existence until 1855.[6] But the measure has been wildly mis-interpreted by successive generations of scholars, who see in it simply a different method to muzzle the press. As Siebert puts it, 'Throughout the eighteenth century, the newspaper stamp, advertisement, and paper taxes operated as an effective control over the periodical press.'[7] A careful examination of the events leading to the institution of a tax on newspapers and pamphlets in 1712, however, reveals the new thinking behind the move. It was the implementation of the Stamp Act which led, ultimately, to the decline in government press controls to this day, and the concomitant rise of tolerance.

I shall return to deal with the events of 1695 and 1712 in more detail in due course. But firstly it will prove necessary to trace

the rise of pre-publication censorship. The first instance of
official censorship of printed matter in England was in the reign
of Henry VIII. In 1530 a proclamation ordered the pre-publication
examination of theological works.[8] Eight years later this was
extended to all books in English. Approval was to be given by the
Royal Licenser before they could be printed. But it was on 4 May
1557, almost exactly eighty years after Caxton began to print at
Westminster, that the privy seal was put to the Charter of
Incorporation of the Stationers' Company, and it was to be this
body that would function as the government agency to regulate
the press. A series of ordinances, injunctions and decrees
cemented the bond between government and its executive machinery.
Authority to search printers' premises and to seize books and
other incriminating evidence was granted to the officers of the
Stationers' Company. Punishment for the failure to enter titles
in the Stationers' Register, or for omitting to submit books for
a license prior to publication, included the destruction of a printer's
press and type; disablement from ever printing again; and six
months' imprisonment without bail. Booksellers and bookbinders
who infringed regulations by working with unlicensed books could
be imprisoned for three months without bail. In 1637, a Star
Chamber decree included clauses ordering all books to be licensed
and entered in the Register at Stationers' Hall, thus endorsing all
previous regulations. Law books were to be scrutinised by one of
the chief justices, and almost every other class of publication by
the Archbishop of Canterbury.

 This, then, was the system which obtained at the outbreak of

civil war, and against which Milton inveighed in <u>Areopagitica</u> as
Popish:[9]

> ...their last invention was to ordain that no Book,
> pamphlet, or paper should be Printed (as if S. Peter
> had bequeath'd them the keys of the Presse also out
> of Paradise) unlesse it were approv'd and licenc't
> under the hands of 2 or 3 glutton Friers... Sometimes
> 5 <u>Imprimaturs</u> are seen together dialogue-wise in the
> Piatza of one Title page, complementing and ducking
> each to other with their shav'n reverences, whether
> the Author, who stands by in perplexity at the foot of
> his Epistle, shall to the Presse or to the spunge. These
> are the prety responsories, these are the deare
> Antiphonies that so bewitcht of late our Prelats, and
> their Chaplaines with the goodly Eccho they made; and
> besotted us to the gay imitation of a lordly <u>Imprimatur</u>,
> one from Lambeth house, another from the <u>West end</u>
> of <u>Pauls</u>; so apishly Romanizing, that the word of
> command still was set downe in Latine; as if the
> learned Grammaticall pen that wrote it, would cast no
> ink without Latine... And thus ye have the Inventors
> and the originall of Book-licencing ript up, and drawn
> as lineally as any pedigree.

Milton was writing in 1644, and he was addressing the parliamen-
tarians. The breakdown of authority had profound effects on the
press. The Long Parliament met in the autumn of 1640. On 5
July 1641 Charles I gave his consent to the abolition of the
Courts of Star Chamber and High Commission. One of the un-
foreseen consequences of this move was the rise of a comparatively
free system of publishing. The monopoly of the Stationers' Company
was undermined when Star Chamber was abolished. The decree of
1637 perished with it. There was, then, no legal necessity to
bother with the Stationers' Company at all - no need to submit
copies for pre-publication scrutiny; no need to enter titles in the

Stationers' Register. If such regulations could not be enforced, then no-one would safeguard the monopoly out of charity. A situation of de facto liberty of the press existed prematurely in the 1640s.

But Parliament soon realised its mistake, as a flood of Royalist propaganda found its way onto the streets. A committee of printing was set up to deal with specific complaints of disorderly publications, and on 14 June 1643 an ordinance for regulating of printing restored to the Stationers' Company its powers of search and seizure, the insistence that all books should be entered in the Stationers' Register, and that copy should be submitted prior to publication for official approval - the old system of licensing, in all its glory, was re-introduced under the auspices not of the monarchy, but of Parliament. Government tolerance of the press was far from becoming a reality. Parliament's inability to control the situation, as more and more newsbooks and pamphlets were published criticising the government, must not be confused with liberal sentiment. In the twenty years of the Great Rebellion, or at least of the Long Parliament, Parliament attempted to censor the press quite as fiercely as the old regime, and, in fact, much more urgently, as the Civil War resulted in a massive upsurge in the numbers of publications, as printers set up presses in defiance of the Stationers' Company and Parliament. The Thomason collection of pamphlets in the British Library includes only twenty-two items published in 1640: in each of the next four years there are over 1,000 titles, and the peak of 1,966 was reached in the year of the outbreak of hostilities, 1642. There

was a similar increase in the production of newsbooks. In 1641
a mere nine of these were published. The following year the
figure had shot up to 167, with corresponding leaps to the record
number of 722 in 1645. In the process, one-off newsbooks were
succeeded by regular publications anticipating the periodical
papers of the reign of Queen Anne.[10]

The official answer to this serious problem was strict censorship. The scale of the phenomenon was such that this proved
impossible to carry out rigorously in practice, but the attitude
is important to record. Milton's impassioned plea against the
licensing system was not heeded. He called instead for a system
of compulsory imprints, each title-page bearing the names of
author, printer and bookseller, and their addresses. In this way
pre-publication censorship would be superseded, and good,
staunch parliamentarian supporters would not be subjected to the
indignity of having their copy scrutinised prior to publication.
Royalist publications, of course, could be treated with the same
severity that Star Chamber had meted out to publications
criticising the King prior to 1641. Milton's liberalism has often
been markedly overstated.

The Great Rebellion, then, had no permanent effect on
government attitudes towards the press. In fact the experience
of dealing for the first time with large amounts of propaganda
censuring authority had a decidedly detrimental effect on the
freedom of the press. True, pre-publication censorship had
existed for over a century, and the Marprelate tracts had defied
printing regulations in 1588 and 1589, but the number of printed

publications had hitherto been quite small. The potentially
revolutionary situation in the 1640s presented a totally new
phenomenon. Censorship was the only answer which offered
itself. One might be justified in saying that the growth of government restrictions, rather than the growth of government tolerance,
is the first part of the story of the 150 years from 1640 to 1790,
and, indeed, Siebert's study is subtitled 'The Rise and Decline
of Government Control'. Attitudes were certainly fixed against
the liberty of the press. In 1649 an Act for the 'better regulating
of Printing' included the 'same old regulations', and the 'same
old prohibitions and punishments', as Cyprian Blagden, the
historian of the Stationers' Company, puts it.[11] Again the same
regulations were enforced, but with final responsibility placed
on the Council of State.

One of the most interesting aspects of the attempt to curb the
flow of political literature during the Civil War period is that
newsbooks bore the brunt of the attack. Clearly it was the accurate
reporting of facts that was regarded as most dangerous. Censorship
in the most pervasive sense was being organised. The 1649 Act
called for the silencing of all newsbooks, whether or not they had
previously been licensed. Henceforth only books and pamphlets
could be published, bearing the names of both the author and the
licenser. Under Cromwell, all newsbooks were suppressed without exception, official and unofficial, licensed and unlicensed
alike. Information was not to be given freely in print. But, of
course, even Cromwell's authority was insufficient 'completely
to prevent...the printing of criticism'.[12] We can simply see the

trend towards a police state, the exact opposite of what Boswell
admired so much about the constitution in the late eighteenth
century. Attitudes had still to be changed to any significant
degree.

Cyprian Blagden has admirably summarised the effects of the
breakdown of authority on the press, and his description is suited
to the reaction to any lapse of government control, whether in
1641, in 1679, or in 1695:[13]

> One of the immediate results of the removal of the
> Court of Star Chamber was the increase in the number,
> the courage and the power of the printers. The main
> opposition parties were able to provide money to
> replace types and presses which had been confiscated
> and rooms to serve as printing-houses; and there were
> hawkers willing to earn a quick penny by selling direct
> to eager purchasers in house and street. This by-
> passing of the booksellers' shops, the normal channels
> of distribution, not only deprived the booksellers of
> business but gave the printers a welcome sense of
> independence. They felt strong enough to break, more
> blatantly than before and often with impunity, the rules
> of their Company.

This optimistic mood was captured in the agitation for a printers'
charter on the Restoration of Charles II in 1660. Would government
attitudes towards the press change, and break the monopoly of the
Stationers' Company once more? No. On 19 May 1662 'An Act
for preventing the frequent Abuses in printing seditious... Books
...and for regulating of Printing and Printing Presses' received
the royal assent. 'The clock was put firmly back to 1637.'[14]
Sir Roger L'Estrange, as Surveyor of the Press under Charles II,
insisted on the Stationers' Company's fulfilment of its duties with

regard to the publication of unlicensed literature. There had been
no breakthrough: if anything, the censorship of the press was now
more rigorous than ever.

Until the Glorious Revolution, then, and beyond, with one short
lapse from 1679 to 1685 (when Charles II was forced to try to
control the press by wielding his prerogative[15]), the publication
of political literature was regulated by law. Each pamphlet and
newspaper had to be submitted to the licenser prior to publication.
Without his seal of approval it was automatically liable to prosecution. Despite temporary relaxations of the press regulations,
the situation which obtained in 1694 was exactly the same in
essence as that which had obtained in 1640. In 1694, however, the
Licensing Act was due to expire. There was nothing unusual in
this. It was the expiry of the 1662 Act in 1679 which led to
Charles II issuing proclamations about the press, in lieu of
applicable legislation. Quite simply, Parliament had forgotten,
or had neglected, to renew the regulations. James II had kept
the licensing system, and so had William III. In 1693 the Act
had come up for renewal, and it had accordingly been renewed
until 1695. But this time it was not renewed. Instead it was
allowed to lapse, and, with the dissolution of William III's second
Parliament in March 1695, pre-publication censorship of the
press in England ceased.[16]

As it happens, censorship of this kind in England had ended
for good (at least let us hope so). But it would be imprudent to
conclude that there had suddenly been a marked change in
attitude towards the press, either on the part of government, or

Parliament, or even public opinion. The expiry of regulations
does not necessarily denote more than parliamentary mismanage-
ment, for, after all, there were no party whips at this time. Our
almost unspoken assumption that there should be a free press was
not even a spoken belief in 1695, and Boswell's comment, which
effectively marks the beginning of the era in which it became an
unspoken assumption to approve of the liberty of the press, was
still a century away. No, the failure to renew the licensing
system in 1694 was due more to doubts about the efficacy of the
measure than to abstract principle. In other words, the pre-
publication censorship of books ended in 1695 not because it was
felt to be wrong, but because the provisions of the Act were not
sufficiently stringent. When the Act was renewed on 3 March
1693, it was only after some consideration of its effectiveness in
preventing the publication of libellous pamphlets. More and more
tracts were being published without a licence. Most of these were
Jacobite, which, of course, would prevent their being approved
if submitted for official scrutiny. Whigs in particular were outraged at the freedom with which Jacobite publications could be
disseminated virtually without redress. Proclamations intended
to suppress libels were issued to end the influx of Jacobite
propaganda - a signal illustration of the plight of the Stationers'
Company at this time. The impartiality of the licensers themselves was openly questioned. Edmund Bohun was of undoubted
Tory sympathy. When the Licensing Act was renewed in 1693,
eleven Lords objected that it subjected 'all learning and true
information to the arbitrary will and Pleasure of a mercenary,

and perhaps ignorant, Licenser; destroys the Properties of
Authors in their Copies; and sets up many monopolies'.[17] Echoes
of Milton's Areopagitica can be detected here; but the reasons are
founded on technical points, not on an abstract theory of the freedom
of the press.

Another great figure entered the lists at this juncture - John
Locke. He campaigned in private, through his political connections,
for the amendment of the Licensing Act when it came up for
renewal in 1694. Again, personal considerations are involved.
His tract, The Reasonableness of Christianity, was not the sort
of thing to be readily approved by a Church Licenser. On 30
November 1694 a committee of the House of Commons was
appointed to examine expired and expiring laws, including the
Licensing Act.[18] It reported a resolution to renew the Licensing
Act six weeks later, but changed its mind on 11 February 1695.
Instead a committee was set up 'to prepare and bring in a Bill
for better regulating of Printing and Printing Presses'.[19] There
is no indication that either the Court or the Church was opposed
to the renewal of the Act. William III had previously made it a
capital offence in Holland to accuse him of aspiring to sovereignty,
and he kept one man, John Rothe, in prison from 1677 to 1691
to silence his pen. Rothe, interestingly enough, was declared to
be insane: an explanation of his continued outspokenness against
the Prince of Orange's regime which has obvious twentieth-
century parallels.[20] The government in the 1690s was not the
sort to back liberal moves towards the liberty of the press.

The proposed new bill was particularly strict in its projected

measures. Pre-publication censorship was reasserted, together
with a system of compulsory imprints - a double safeguard, if
you like. Anyone whose name appeared in an imprint would be
answerable as if he were the author of the book. Powers of
search and seizure were to be confirmed, but, significantly, the
monopoly of the Stationers' Company was to end. It would be
reasonable to assume that this draft bill put forward the attitudes
of the government towards the press. It sought to tie up loop-
holes; not to tear fresh holes in the fabric of government control.
Every sheet of print was to be carefully scrutinised before being
passed for publication. But the amended bill came to nought. The
Stationers' Company, not surprisingly, raised objections. Then
the House of Lords included the old Licensing Act in the composite
reviving bill sent up from the Commons, from which it had been
deliberately omitted. After a conference between the two houses,
the bill was dropped once more. The result was the lapse of pre-
publication censorship.

Macaulay's frustration at this point becomes unbearable: 'On
the great question of principle, on the question whether the
liberty of unlicensed printing be, on the whole, a blessing or a
curse to society, not a word is said.' Hardly surprising, seeing
that the issue was one of effective censorship, and of the legal
rights of authors, printers, and the Stationers' Company. Locke,
like Milton half a century before, was ahead of his time, and, it
should be stressed, not as liberal in his theories as has often
been suggested. But the matter was far from settled. With hindsight, Macaulay was correct to celebrate the end of pre-publication

censorship: 'English literature was emancipated, and emancipated for ever, from the control of government.'[21] This would not have seemed the case to men living in the late seventeenth and early eighteenth centuries. Our task now is to explain why restrictions were not re-imposed, and, much more important to the rise of a genuinely free press, how government attitudes altered to permit such a growth.

In the first place it should be emphasised that it was not for want of trying that regulations were not re-imposed. A new bill was launched at the very start of William III's third Parliament in November 1695, and successive bills, many of them involving little more than a return to the licensing system, were proposed, the last in 1712. None became law. Instead government was reduced to proclaiming impotently against the licentiousness of the press. Why? The expiry of the Licensing Act, together with the Triennial Act, passed in December 1694, which necessitated a new Parliament every three years, led to a tremendous growth in literature, particularly of a political nature.[22] As in 1641, when Star Chamber was abolished, and 1679, when the licensing system previously lapsed at the height of the exclusion crisis, the sudden absence of restrictions unleashed the fury of the party presses. Now only ambiguous laws, similar to those operating today, were the means of checking the forces of rhetoric. Pamphlets of a treasonous, blasphemous or seditious nature could be prosecuted. And, in theory, new titles were still to be registered in the records of the Stationers' Company. But without any enforcement machinery, relatively few titles are to

be found in the Stationers' Register after 1695.

The first significant development after the ending of censorship was the appearance of newspapers, and it was this knowledge of affairs that the government was most concerned to prevent. The springing up of newspapers almost overnight in 1695 was one of the main reasons that the reintroduction of censorship was strongly championed. The attitude was long-lived. A few far-sighted individuals, however, began to recognise the potential of printed propaganda to influence public opinion, and to achieve specific political objectives. Of course the opposition had always taken the opportunity, whenever it had offered itself, to criticise government policy and ministerial conduct. The crucial change occurred when the organisation of government propaganda matched, and then surpassed, the output and efficacy of opposition propaganda. Clearly the process was a complex one, but the pioneers can be recognised. John, Lord Somers of the Junto organised government propaganda during the standing army controversy from 1697 to 1699. Then, from 1700, and, in parti-cular, from 1702 and the accession of Anne, Robert Harley took the organisation of ministerial propaganda into his own hands.

The impetus for this changed ministerial attitude towards the press came largely from Robert Harley, who was created Earl of Oxford and Mortimer in 1711, appointed Lord Treasurer in the same month, and who, from 1710 to 1714, was Prime Minister in all but title. Under his auspices a government press policy began to emerge - one, moreover, that did not rely overwhelmingly on censorship, or even the proscription of troublesome opposition pamphleteers. True, Harley apprehended, prosecuted and punished a number of authors and printers, particularly as Secretary of State from 1704 to 1708. Defoe, for instance, was pilloried three times in 1703 for his The Shortest Way with the Dissenters, and Harley was involved in the prosecution. The significant fact is that, instead of keeping Defoe in gaol – he was imprisoned during Her Majesty's Pleasure – Harley set him free, laying obligations upon him, such as standing surety for his good behaviour, and got him to work as a government apologist. In 1704 Harley launched Defoe's Review, a paper 'to state facts right', as he put it. [23] If information was to be available, it might as well be the 'official' version of things. In 1702 all ministerial printed matter was carried by the official newspaper, The London Gazette. By 1713 the Ministry boasted five press organs: the Gazette, the Review, the Examiner, the Post Boy, and the Mercator. These outnumbered the opposition papers of the Whigs. Harley supervised the setting up of distribution agencies, facilitating the speedy and efficient dissemination of government propaganda throughout the kingdom, and, largely through the offices of Jonathan Swift, he made arrangements with printers.

It is not often that Harley's contribution to the rise of a free press in England is pointed out, but it was crucial to the superseding of the system of pre-publication censorship. Under Harley, the necessity of government control was replaced by an arrangement which exploited the advantages government possessed to subsidise printed propaganda. Only when government was in a position to gain more through the encouragement of an apparently free press, were the conditions conducive to the rise of a genuinely free press able to come about. Harley's organisation of government propaganda was an important step in this direction. Secondly, there was the question of the legal status of the press. After the expiry of the Licensing Act in 1695, the next legislation relating to the press (excluding the copyright act of 1709) occurred when Harley was leading the administration in 1712 as Earl of Oxford. It is conventional to comment upon the government's 'repressive campaign' at this juncture. This is supposed to have culminated in the Stamp Act, which was clearly a 'new repressive measure'.[24] In fact the Stamp Act served to put an end to the notion of press regulations, and is vital to the growth of government tolerance.

It might be useful to illustrate the way in which the Stamp Act has been misinterpreted. The Queen's message to the House of Commons of 17 January 1712 is commonly believed to have led to the institution of the hated tax on newspapers and pamphlets. After all, it suggested that the 'evil' of the licentiousness of the press had 'grown too strong for the laws now in force'. A 'remedy equal to the mischief' was called for. It has been assumed that this 'remedy' was the Stamp Act, projected with the hope that a tax would prove prohibitive to the Whig propagandists. A new measure, maybe, but a repressive one. And yet, if so, why was the duty on each newspaper cut from a penny to a halfpenny in the committee stage of the bill? If the idea really was to stamp out political publications in the course of stamping the paper on which they were printed, surely it would have been better to have doubled the duty, instead of halving it? Jonathan Swift was unenthusiastic

about the Stamp Act, but in favour of a restrictive system of
press controls. His attitude is worth considering as typical of
those championing regulations. He expected the government 'to
have proposed some ways by which th[e] evil of the licentiousness
of the press might be removed, the law for taxing papers having
produced a quite contrary effect, as was then foreseen by many
persons and hath since been found true by experience'.[25] On
another occasion Swift noted that 'a bill for a much more effectual
regulation[of the press]was brought into the House of Commons
[in 1712], but so late in the session that there was no time to pass
it...However it came about this affair was put off from one week
to another, and the bill not brought into the house till the 8th of
June. It was committed three days later, and then heard of no
more.'[26]

Existing histories of the English press make no mention of
this bill. In fact they confuse two entirely separate proposals
when they refer to the repressive character of the Stamp Act.
On 12 April 1712 a Committee of the whole House met to consider
the Queen's message. The report was due to be read on 15 April;
instead, as Swift remarks, it 'was put off from one week to
another'. In reality it was put off no less than seven times. It
called for the registration of all printing presses, and advised
the House that 'to every book, pamphlet, and paper, which shall
be printed, there be set the name, and the place of abode of the
author, printer, and publisher thereof'.[27] But, as Swift noted,
the bill was lost after its second reading when Parliament was
prorogued on 8 July 1712. In the meantime a duty on printed

paper had been introduced, and it had proceeded onto the statute-
books. It should be emphasised that, when the Committee of the
whole House debated the Queen's message on 12 April, the question
of a tax on printed matter had not been considered. The report of
the committee was due to be heard on 22 April. It had already
been postponed once. It was put off again. Instead, on the same
day, the Committee of Ways and Means reported several resolutions concerning stamp duties on paper. A tax was proposed on
'all pamphlets and newspapers, printed or written'. This passed
the Commons, could not be turned down by the Lords, and
received the royal assent on 22 May 1712. It pre-empted the bill
for compulsory imprints, which Swift had thought 'a much more
effectual regulation' of the press. By the time the resolutions of
the committee on the Queen's message were reported to the
House, the Stamp Act was law, and it was operational from
1 August 1712.

   Government thinking about the press had altered markedly.
Political management was clearly in evidence in the passing of the
Stamp Act. Far from hoping to ruin Whig periodicals, the government wished to exploit their popularity. The revenue was small,
it is true, but it seems to have been designed to fund a lottery.
When newspapers and pamphlets were discussed in 1711 as things
'upon which money is like to be raised',[28] they were considered
in relation to a lottery.[29] Harley, then, did not want to destroy
the press through the Stamp Act. It was primarily a revenue-
raising device. A secondary consideration was, no doubt, the
fact that it would make things more difficult for the Whigs. But

to the growth of government tolerance of the press, the real importance of the Stamp Act is that it reveals an entirely new attitude, which sought to tax a popular commodity, rather than to silence it completely.

Support for this interpretation of the Stamp Act is provided by a brief examination of its effects. If it was meant to prove prohibitive to Whig literature, it failed. Until recently it has been customary to suggest that the introduction of the tax resulted in a decline in the book trade. This is not the case. Foxon's English Verse 1701-1750, for instance, shows that more poems were published in 1712 and 1713 than before the Stamp Act, and that this trend continued.[30] Similarly, tables produced by Ian Maxted relating to the English book trade in the eighteenth century, 'based on rough counts'[31] from sources like the Monthly Catalogue, Monthly Chronicle, Monthly Review, London Magazine and Gentleman's Magazine, show that in terms of the number of books published per year, the peak, surprisingly, was in 1714, two years after the supposedly detrimental Stamp Act. Of course it is always difficult to decide how to define a 'book' in such cases, yet government did not take steps to curb the publication of literature. Walpole retained Harley's measure. In 1737 he licensed theatrical performances - these had to be vetted by a licenser - but printed matter was allowed to appear unhindered, subject only to the ambiguous laws relating to treason, blasphemy and seditious libel. It was certainly feared that the licensing of plays would be 'a Forerunner' to an attack on the liberty of the press,[32] but in the event Walpole preferred to raise revenue from

the press. Like Harley, he used his intelligence system and
Treasurer's purse to organise the production and distribution of
ministerial propaganda on an effective scale. Looking back, 1712
was indeed the vital date in the growth of government tolerance.

One caveat. After 1715 the political environment cooled down.
The septennial system superseded the triennial, and served to
curb the production of political literature. Political sermons
were banned, and the Riot Act was a strong deterrent to political
demonstrations. Literature was still craved, but the demand took
a somewhat different form. I detect a connection here between the
desire for reading-matter and the rise of the novel, or, more
strictly, an increased market for prose fiction. And yet the
number of novels published between 1700 and 1750 is small, nor
are many published each year even in the second half of the
century when compared to the vastly different book trade of today.
Hence, perhaps, the surprising conclusion to be drawn from
Maxted's tables that more books were published in the early
years of the century than even in the years running up to 1800.
The size of press-runs is an almost unknown quantity in the early
eighteenth century. Ian Watt, in The Rise of the Novel, does not
refer to the expiry of the licensing system, nor to the stamp
duty. I would hazard a guess at the effect of pre-publication
censorship on the rise of the novel. True, it is only an hypothesis,
but I can't see the Archbishop of Canterbury and his officers
readily licensing Moll Flanders, Pamela, or Tom Jones, let
alone Fanny Hill. Perhaps even Robinson Crusoe would have met
with opposition. Unmentioned by Professor Watt, the rise of the

novel owes as much to the lapse of regulations on the press as it does to supply and demand, although the imposition of a tax on printed literature could be interpreted in Marxian terms.

The most crucial development in the growth of government tolerance of the press is, of course, a distinct change in attitude. This can be seen taking place in the years of the Walpole era, as the cry of liberty of the press was raised long and loud by the opposition. Most likely this was a political move, rather than a dearly-held abstract principle, but the very fact that such a belief was aired illustrates the advance. When the lapse of the Licensing Act was under discussion in 1695, or when the introduction of the Stamp Act was being debated in Parliament and in print in 1712, very few mentions were made of the desirability of a free press. True, the odd voice did mouth the principle, but more breath was spent on technical matters relating to the book trade – the monopoly of the Stationers' Company, the rights of the author, copyright, etc., and the plight of those who made their livings out of the book trade. The publications of the motley opposition to Walpole, however, made free use of the liberty of the press platform. The journal called The True Briton, launched by the outspoken Jacobite, Philip, Duke of Wharton on 3 June 1723, stressed, in the very first issue, that 'THE Freedom of the PRESS, is another Bulwark of our Liberty; and there needs no greater Arguments to prove it, than the frequent Attempts that have been made to destroy it, under Pretence of Restraining of it. Wicked Men must naturally labour to have their Actions conceal'd, or, at least, so published, that every Person should credit the Glosses which they themselves throw upon them...' Macaulay's vision is at last being fulfilled, after a gap of thirty years. Now, for some reason, the freedom of the press is a 'Bulwark of our Liberty' - it is awarded a new-found status in the face of the corruption and blatant attempts to influence public opinion of the Walpolean regime. The paper of the opposition surrounding Henry St John, Viscount Bolingbroke, The Craftsman, also included a cry for freedom in its second number in 1726: 'By the Liberty of the Press I mean (as I suppose every body else does) an unreserved, discretionary power for every man to publish his thoughts on any subject, and in any manner, which is not expressly forbidden by the Laws of the Land, without being obliged to apply for a licence or privilege for so doing.'

By the second decade of the eighteenth century the idea of pre-publication censorship was irrevocably damned. Bolingbroke, who had probably been the champion of regulations in 1712,[33] used the platform of press liberty to embarrass Walpole. He even printed the objections of the House of Commons to the renewal of the Licensing Act in 1695 in The Craftsman in 1731, with the rider that they had been drawn up by the 'great Mr. Locke'.[34] To Bolingbroke, licensing now symbolised 'the arbitrary Power of the Court and their Creatures' - a predictable application in view of his hatred of the Walpole ministry.

Despite the introduction of licensing regulations regarding the theatre in 1737 and the fears of the opposition, Walpole did not offer any official answer to the printed criticism of his regime. However unwillingly, government tolerated most aspects of the press. There was one big exception to this general liberty, and

it was this issue which was resolved as a result of Wilkite agitation
in the 1760s and 1770s. There were sanctions against the publication of parliamentary debates, and until these were removed,
there was still some way to go before Boswell's ideal was realised.
It is for this reason that parliamentary diaries kept by individual
M.P.s such as Anchitell Grey, Narcissus Luttrell and Sir Edward
Knatchbull are invaluable. The reporting of proceedings in
Parliament was a breach of privilege, and dealt with as such. Of
course it became increasingly difficult to distinguish between
parliamentary tolerance of the press and government tolerance.
A Commons' resolution, for instance, of 26 February 1728,
confirmed the principle. Walpole's hand was detected by the
opposition behind the move, as an attempt to withold information
about the conduct of the people's representatives in Parliament.
Other resolutions were made, by the Commons in 1738, and by
the Lords in 1747 relating to the trial of the Jacobite, Lord Lovat.

In the 1730s, then, Samuel Johnson was forced to cultivate
anonymity as a reporter of parliamentary debates for The Gentleman's
Magazine. It was only in the 1760s that, accompanying the Wilkite
agitations, the practice of reporting debates in the press markedly
increased. The Bill of Rights Society, no doubt much to Macaulay's
delight, sponsored the development. In 1771 the Society joined in
the fight to defend the printers of London against the House of
Commons. Early in the year the House made a determined attempt
to halt the publication of its proceedings. As the Middlesex Journal
puts it: 'It was reported, that a scheme was at last hit upon by the
ministry to prevent the public from being informed of their

iniquity.'[35] The public reaction to the Commons' resolution was
the logical consequence of the gradual demand for the free avail-
ability of information, from the newsbooks of the 1640s, through
the rise of newspapers after the expiry of the Licensing Act, to
the opposition allegations that Walpole was deliberately silencing
the nation's representatives in Parliament: 'nay', The Craftsman
had thundered,

> we have seen some great men stoop so low, as to collogue
> with common News-writers and Journalists, in order to
> obstruct all avenues to Truth, and induce them, by bribes,
> to serve their corrupt purposes with fictitious intelligence
> and false representations.
>   From this negative state of the question, we may judge
> when the Liberty of the Press really subsists in any
> nation; for where such methods are practised, in any
> degree, there can be no such Liberty; since a privilege
> which is invaded and superceded, in this manner, is
> no privilege at all; it is indeed only the names of
> departed Liberty...

The call for the free publication of parliamentary debates was the
final step in the campaign for a free press, and it is appropriate
that the supporters of Wilkes and liberty should have been its
champions. The Commons' initiative was wrecked by Wilkite
aldermen of the City of London. In their capacity as magistrates
they used the judicial privileges of the City to block attempts to
enforce parliamentary privilege. On one occasion a Commons'
messenger was charged with assault for attempting to arrest John
Miller, of the London Evening Post. The messenger was released
only after bail had been provided by the Deputy Serjeant-at-Arms
of the House of Commons. On 14 March 1771 several printers
promised, at the bar of the House, to stop publishing reports of

debates. They quickly began again, but the Commons felt it more
prudent to rest on this technical triumph, and from then onwards
the practice of reporting parliamentary proceedings went on
unhindered. Finally, in the 1780s, reporters were actually allowed
to take notes in the House. Previously they had been forced to rely
solely on memory for accuracy. The principle so dear to Boswell
had, by 1790, been won: 'In our time [the press] has acquired an
unrestrained freedom, so that the people in all parts of the
kingdom have a fair, open, and exact report of the actual proceedings
of their representatives and legislators, which in our constitution
is highly to be valued. '

From the situation in 1640, then, when Star Chamber decrees
enforced the pre-publication censorship organised by the
Stationers' Company, the press had gained the position in which
it operates today. Almost. The final government check was
removed in 1792 with Fox's Libel Act. Now governments could
indeed bring in charges of treason, blasphemy or seditious libel
against individual publications, but the cases were tried openly
by jury. And, in 1855, the Stamp Act, introduced in 1712,
ceased to function. But taxation is, in principle, a different sort
of restraint from censorship per se. By 1790 the press had at
least been granted official approval. This stemmed from events
in 1695 and 1712. The expiry of the Licensing Act permitted the
growth of political literature in the reign of Queen Anne, and it
was, paradoxically, the virulence of the political press that led
to its freedom. Not that the propagandists of these years were
preoccupied with the liberty of the press. Rather, it was Robert

Harley's determination to organise propaganda which forestalled
the reintroduction of press regulations. And it was the popularity
of the press which gave rise to schemes to raise revenue through
its taxation. So, curiously enough, purely practical considerations
were instrumental in the growth of government tolerance of the
press. Harley's motives may not have been admirable. They may
smack more of filtering information to manipulate public opinion.
But in the long run it was propaganda which resulted in the
tolerance of the press. The Stamp Act did not destroy the book
trade. Instead, it signalled the demise of official censorship.
Expediency is always more effective than principle in the political
arena.

Notes

1. L. Hanson, Government and the Press, 1695-1763, Oxford, 1936.

2. F.S. Siebert, Freedom of the Press in England 1476-1776: The Rise and Decline of Government Control, Urbana, Illinois, 1965.

3. R. Astbury, 'The Renewal of the Licensing Act in 1693 and its Lapse in 1695', The Library, fifth series, xxxiii (1978), 296-322.

4. J.A. Downie, Robert Harley and the Press: Propaganda and Public Opinion in the Age of Swift and Defoe, Cambridge, 1979, pp. 149-61.

5. J. Boswell, The Life of Samuel Johnson, with a Journal of a Tour to the Hebrides, ed. G.B. Hill, revised by L.F. Powell, 6 vols., Oxford, 1934-50, i.115-16.

6. Siebert, Freedom of the Press, p.322.

7. Ibid.

8. I am indebted to two works for the summary of the history of press regulations which follows: Siebert, Freedom of the Press, and Cyprian Blagden, The Stationers' Company, London, 1960.

9. E. Sirluck ed., Complete Prose Works of John Milton: Volume II: 1643-1648, New Haven and London, 1959, pp. 505-6.

10. See Siebert, Freedom of the Press, pp. 191n., 203n.

11. Blagden, The Stationers' Company, p. 146.

12. Ibid. p. 147.

13. Ibid.

14. Ibid. p. 148.

15. For a recent account, see Timothy Crist, 'Government Control of the Press after the Expiration of the Printing Act in 1679', Publishing History, v (1979), 49-77.

16. For details of the expiry of the Licensing Act, I am indebted to Astbury, 'The Renewal of the Licensing Act'.

17. Astbury, 'The Renewal of the Licensing Act', p. 302.

18. Journals of the House of Commons, xi, 180.

19. Ibid. pp. 200, 213, 218, 224, 228. See Astbury, 'The Renewal of the Licensing Act', p. 309.

20. Ibid. p. 306.

21. T. B. Macaulay, A History of England to the Death of William III, ed. C. H. Firth, London, 1913, v, 2482.

22. For an extended treatment of the issues discussed in the following paragraphs, see Downie, Robert Harley and the Press.

23. British Library Add. MS 28055, fol. 3: Harley to the Earl of Godolphin, 9 August 1702.

24. D. H. Stevens, Party Politics and English Journalism 1702-1742, Menasha, Wisconsin, 1916, p. 33; Irvin Ehrenpreis, Swift: The Man, His Works, and the Age: Volume II: Dr Swift, London, 1967, p. 568.

25. H. Davis ed., The Prose Writings of Jonathan Swift, Oxford, 1939-75, vii. 103-4.

26. Ibid. p. 105.

27. Journals of the House of Commons, xvii, 28, 175, 185, 191, 198, 204, 210, 220, 247, 251.

28. British Library Loan 29/280, fol. 80.

29. N. Luttrell, A Brief Historical Relation of State Affairs from September 1678 to April 1714, Oxford, 1857, vi. 680-1.

30. D. F. Foxon, English Verse 1701-1750: A Catalogue of Separately Printed Poems with Notes on Contemporary

Collected Editions, Cambridge, 1975, ii. 81-8.

31.I. Maxted, The London Book Trades 1775-1800, London, 1977, p. xxxi.

32.Daily Journal, 25 March 1737. See Thomas Lockwood, 'A New Essay by Fielding', Modern Philology, 77 (1980), 54.

33.See Downie, Robert Harley and the Press, pp. 153-4.

34.The Craftsman, no. 281, 20 November 1731, cited in Astbury, 'The Renewal of the Licensing Act', p. 315n.

35.The details of the Wilkite contribution to the rise of a free press are taken from P.D.G. Thomas, 'John Wilkes and the Freedom of the Press, 1771', Bulletin of the Institute of Historical Research, 33 (1960), 86-98.

Periodicals and the Book Trade

Michael Harris

On 8 November 1754, William Sandby, bookseller at the sign of
the ship opposite St. Dunstan's Church, Fleet Street, sat down to
dinner at the nearby Horn Tavern with half-a-dozen colleagues
and friends. [1] In itself such an occasion is a matter of limited, if
poignant, interest reflecting the traditional conviviality of
'respectable' London booksellers which shows up so clearly on
the benign features of John Nichols. [2] Its interest, in the context
of this short paper, arises from the group's underlying interest
as shareholders in the General Evening Post and hence of the
indication it provides of developments in the trade which already
in the mid-eighteenth century had hardened into a classic management structure.

The term 'book trade', used in the title, is itself ambiguous,
embracing a vast range of interlocking activity: from type-
founders and paper-makers to hack authors, from prosperous
business men to destitute entrepreneurs, and from complicated
commercial structures to low-key personal operations. However,
in considering shifts in the relationships within this complicated
hierarchy the periodical provides a serviceable means of access.
The London newspaper, in particular, represents a point at which

a whole range of interests coincide and are brought into sharp
relief.

At the opening of the eighteenth century the book trade, as long-
established, found itself confronted with a new set of challenges.
The lapse of the Licensing Act in 1695, though hardly in itself a
spectacular event, had brought the whole apparatus of control
crashing down.[3] In the printing trade, individuals, with no formal
training or connection with the suddenly emasculated Stationers'
Company, began to set up on their own account taking in one, two
or more apprentices.[4] Partly through the resultant overcrowding
and partly through an eye to the main chance, individuals in the
trade began to remove from London to previously outlawed
provincial towns, setting up in Bristol, Norwich, and other
major centres of population. William Bonney was in the van of
this process, moving to Bristol at the end of 1694 and thus
achieving a considerable commercial coup de main.[5] Although
Bonney does not appear initially to have been involved in periodical
publication, the drift of printers to the provinces can be charted
through the appearance of a sequence of local newspapers. In
London itself, a symptom of the removal of control (as in 1679
when the License had temporarily lapsed)[6] was an upsurge in
the production of periodicals which, as well as providing a reasonably
secure base for a printing business (a point I shall return to later),
had a well established appeal for the vast London readership. Much
of the output on which the expansion in the printing trade was based
had a political flavour and it was hardly surprising that established
members of the trade, facing a rising tide of competition, should

have looked for ministerial support for the construction of a new
method of control. Petitions and memorials from within the trade
urging the resurrection of the License and offering suggestions of
alternative means of oversight recur in the early years of the
century, providing a counterpoint to the political moves which
culminated in the Stamp Act of 1712.[7] As a measure aimed
primarily at the newspaper this could have been seen as a step
towards trade regulation.

The lapse of the Act in 1695 struck home elsewhere in the book
business as it removed the only formal protection of copyright in
England.[8] The real profits to be made by the London booksellers
lay less in the retail business done over the shop counter than in
the ownership of copies. Between about 1680 and 1780 this pre-
dominant fact of financial life provided the main stimulus to
change within the upper levels of the book trade. The lapse in
protective legislation intensified the problem and threw the booksellers back on their own resources. With the Stationers'
Company exercised to defend its own literary monopolies and
with the recourse to common law providing a very limited and
expensive means of redress, the impetus towards mutual
self-defence was given an effective shove. In some ways the
product itself, the book, created an inherent tendency towards
quite sophisticated group organisation. The number of individuals
involved in the total process from production to distribution
implied a commercial structure of some intricacy. Equally, the
need for often high initial investment which might not yield a
profit for a long period gave an obvious push towards partnership

and shared risks. The imprints of a cross-section of books
published in the early eighteenth century testify to the extent and
variety of book trade co-operation. To these positive incentives
was added the increasingly problematic negative influence of
piracy. This element of original sin in production and publication
was emphasised after 1695 when the removal of front-line restraint
offered up rare possibilities to the unscrupulous. Henry Hills, with
his 'under the counter' business in sermons and poems, was only
one of the more notorious individuals who built up a business on
the strength of other peoples' literary property.[9] Well before the
lapse members of the London trade had come up with an extension
of the partnership arrangements which was pregnant with impli-
cations for the future. From about 1690 a group of some fifteen
London booksellers formed themselves into a loose association,
referred to in the trade as 'the Conger'. This self-explanatory
reference to conger eels was taken up by the sceptical individualist
John Dunton: 'What kind of a Fish is a Conger?' he asked, 'Why
'tis an overgrown Eel, that devours all the Food from the weaker
Grigs, and when he wants other Food, swallows them too into
the bargain.'[10] For the next thirty years this shifting group of
individuals initiated or developed a set of trade practices involving
common ownership of books, price-fixing, publicity and, perhaps
most importantly, exercising some degree of pragmatic control
by personal influence over any challenge to their copies. The
Copyright Act of 1709/10 checked blatant piracy but was characteristically inadequate in either the short or long term.[11] The low
level of fines which it embodied, as well as the limited period of

ownership which it endorsed, were ultimately to lead to the
ferocious struggle over literary property which developed later
in the century. [12] In the meantime the booksellers, led by 'the
Conger', were proving capable of looking after their own interests.
During the first twenty years of the century a series of formal
and informal groups came into being, creating at least a temporary
stability in the field of copyright. The 'Printing Conger' and the
'Castle (or New) Conger' represented a growing capacity for the
development of more efficient organisation. One indication of an
increasing expertise is provided by the emergence of a system
of ownership-transfer embodied in the trade sales at which shares
in literary property were sold by auction. The two major sets of
records covering these events were kept by the firms of Ward
and Longman, the earliest entries in both dating from 1718. [13]
Some element of share trading undoubtedly took place at an
earlier time, but the coincidence of this date with heightened
commercial activity in the field of joint-stock enterprise
generally may reflect an interaction between the book trade and
more diverse areas of commercial activity.

These two lines of development - the expansion of the printing
trade and the extension of group co-operation among 'respectable'
booksellers - meet in the periodical and in particular in the newspaper. While such publications could offer the printer a good
financial deal, they also provided the booksellers generally with
a variety of useful services. Books, pamphlets and the whole
gamut of booksellers' output had been advertised in periodicals
from the mid-seventeenth century and there is little question but

that maintaining a reasonable level of business required the sort
of promotion that only newspaper advertising could provide. On
the other hand, and at a rather different level, the supply of
newspapers to customers as well as to distributors in the
provinces, must have provided a useful means of stimulating the
more haphazard and occasional business of selling books;
cementing contacts which could lead to additional orders. It
appears that most London booksellers, however prosperous,
were involved in newspaper distribution. Bills presented by
Benjamin Motte, William Innys and Jacob Tonson to the executors
of ex-customers contain multiple entries of leading newspapers
between the books which formed the staple of their business.[14]
The way in which the newspaper mediated in bookseller/customer
relations appears most clearly in a ledger of Robert Gosling
covering the 1730s. Most customers were in receipt of London
newspapers and in many cases were using Gosling as an inter-
mediary in placing advertisements in the London press on a
variety of subjects.[15] The links between the London booksellers
and their provincial counterparts are more obscure but in the
complicated process of distribution, periodicals were probably
useful grist.

In these ways alone the booksellers had a long-term interest
in newspapers which could be threatened by a variety of circumstances. Quirks of ownership, personal quarrels, casual shifts
in policy could interrupt or cut off access to one or more key
papers. Equally, sheer lack of space in the most effective forms
of publication might frustrate a major advertising campaign.

This sort of consideration probably underlay the move by groups
of booksellers into the area of joint ownership of newspapers
which, though taking place at a low level of visibility, seems to
have been well under way by 1720. The first groups may have
been formed by extended participation in such established papers
as the Daily Courant whose shares appear early on in the trade
sale records. Perhaps the first papers to be set up under full-
scale joint ownership were the Daily Post and the Daily Journal,
published in 1718 and 1719 respectively.[17] These were the first
new dailies to appear in the capital since the Courant at the
beginning of the century, and were clearly seen as a means of
opening up the London market. The identity of the proprietors
and their relationship as individuals or as groups to existing
'Congers' has yet to be worked out. It seems likely that the
shareholders were made up of freely associating individuals who
may have been involved in some common publishing enterprises
and who occasionally shared some mutual political attitudes. Politics
is never, after all, to be ruled out as an adjunct to financial
speculation[18] (the Daily Post took an opposition and the Daily
Journal a ministerial line). From 1720 such groups were
increasingly involved in the ownership of the major forms of
London newspaper. The thrice-weeklies with a national distribution
and a unique potential for provincial advertising rapidly appeared
under bookseller ownership. The London Evening Post and General
Evening Post were financed by the booksellers and soon superseded
their long-established rivals. During the late 1720s and early 1730s
groups of booksellers underwrote a series of weekly papers with

a more or less literary leading-essay including the Grub Street
Journal which outlived most of its competitors and has provided,
through the random survival of its shareholders minutes, one of
the few indications of how bookseller ownership worked in practice.[19]
In fact the limitations of the weekly paper, both as a vehicle for
advertising and as a source of income, ultimately led the booksellers to withdraw, leaving this form of publication to the printers
and the politicians.

A general absence of solid documentary evidence leaves much
of the process well below the surface and it will take interminable
efforts by generations of researchers before a full and accurate
assessment of the precise extent of bookseller involvement in the
periodical press can be established. In general it seems that the
number of shareholders in any enterprise varied with its form,
more for the dailies and thrice-weeklies than for the weeklies
and monthlies, and that in general any given newspaper was
likely to have between eight and twenty proprietors.[20] The
personnel of each group was relatively stable, mainly because
each imposed considerable restraint on its members and the sale
of shares was carefully monitored. This accounts for the very
limited number of references to newspaper shares in the Ward/
Longman catalogues. The London booksellers generally were,
for reasons already stated, a very cautious set of people and the
sales were themselves closed to anyone who might interfere with
an orderly transfer among themselves. Provincial booksellers,
printers, pamphlet and print sellers and anyone working in a
related area of business were rigorously excluded.[21] From the

limited evidence it appears that agreement of the rest of the group
was usually required before a transfer could take place, though
some proprietors were permitted to dispose of a moiety of their
holding, and very few non-booksellers appear among the shareholders. As I have suggested elsewhere[22] some relaxation may
have taken place later in the century, but in the first half, the
structure remained carefully sewn up.

The move by the booksellers into the field of periodical
publication apparently represented a significant departure from
the joint ownership of literary copies. The exigencies of the form,
involving the need for a high level of oversight, drew the shareholders into the demanding area of active, general management.
As proprietors the booksellers became continuously involved, at
meetings held monthly or even weekly, in the routine business of
running a periodical, considering not only financial matters and
the level of advertising but the quality of the paper and print, the
currency of the news coverage and the level of interest of supple-
mentary content. How far this went beyond the conventional role
of the 'Congers' handling the more routine business involved in
the production of books remains largely guesswork. How did the
'Congers' operate? How was the extraordinarily intricate
process of shareholding monitored within and between groups?
Who kept the accounts and distributed the profits? Answers to
some of these questions can be extrapolated from the notebooks
of Thomas Bennet and Henry Clements which contains information
on the organisation of the 'Wholesaling Conger'. However, the
limitations of this material and the fragmented character of other

evidence (even when supplemented by the labyrinthine efforts of
Terry Belanger) only serve to underline the comparative solidity
of the organisation of newspaper management. It seems reasonable
to suggest that the extension of periodical ownership tightened up
the infra-structure of the book trade, giving a degree of formality
and practical effectiveness to the booksellers which they had not
previously obtained. The forms of management which had developed
by the 1730s need not concern us in detail though it is of some
interest to note the way in which the evolution of business practice
was drawing the upper levels of the book trade further away from
other forms of commercial activity in London. The internal arrangements and the general framework of meetings, which invariably
included a midsummer jaunt to such country resorts as Greenwich
and Blackheath, resemble forms of local government more closely
than those of other groups of London tradesmen. It is characteristic
that a model for the structure of management can be found outside
the book trade. From 1710 the Sun Fire Insurance Office promoted
its business by the distribution, at reduced cost to clients, of a
newspaper entitled the British Mercury.[24] Initially appearing three
times per week, though revamped from 1712 as a six-page weekly,
it was conducted by a management board made up of Sun Fire
shareholders. These included three printers, John Heptenstall,
Matthew Jennour and Hugh Meere, as well as Thomas Norris,
a bookseller on London Bridge. The meetings at which the
management of the Mercury was discussed were identical in form
and character to those at which the booksellers were to conduct
their newspaper business for the rest of the century.

Attendance at meetings of newspaper proprietors seems to have been erratic and a proportion of the shareholders only went to general meetings or remained as sleeping partners in spite of the varied financial penalties and incentives devised by those who turned up. The concern with keeping an eye on their investment seems to have kept a regular nucleus at work, though occasionally a sort of terminal inertia set in which left the printer entirely to his own devices. The clubbish character of the sessions must have been one element in holding the groups together and the combination of shared literary interests and a regular pattern of good dinners, as I suggested at the start, probably had a role to play. It is characteristic that one of the early 'Congers' took its soubriquet from the Castle Tavern, where meetings were held, and a list of locations at which the newspaper proprietors met would offer a good food guide to eighteenth-century London.[25]

One of the disincentives to taking part in the management process may have been the limited financial role that the newspaper played in the investments of most of the 'respectable' booksellers who held shares. The initial input was modest usually, perhaps, during the first half of the century, £20 or £30 per head with some additional calls during the early stages of publication; and though the value of a single share varied with a newspaper's popularity it was never likely to exceed £100.[26] Equally, dividends, though regular and not to be sneezed at, can seldom have amounted to more than £20 half yearly. Periodical ownership was, therefore, probably less than crucial to such booksellers as Lawton Gilliver and John Nourse, though perhaps

more to the former as a prime mover in the Grub Street Journal.
Control was the vital ingredient and a line into the management of
a paper was probably worth at least as much to most proprietors
as the potential return.

Elsewhere in the book trade the periodical had a more important,
not to say vital, financial role. Although it had become a commonplace by the mid-1730s to complain of a bookseller monopoly of
the periodical press, such comments were based on a gross
oversimplification. To the London printer a periodical, in particular a newspaper, remained the potential basis of successful
business. For a low initial investment a paper could provide
regular work with a continuous and easily monitored return. The
boom in periodicals at the opening of the century had given a clear
indication of their value in keeping printers afloat in a time of
crisis, and the newspaper remained an aid to commercial mobility,
a ladder by which individuals at a low level of activity could escape
from the vicious circle of drudgery and poverty. The example of
printers who had built up their business on the strength of a
successful newspaper was constantly available. Nathaniel Mist,
James Read and John Applebee, though also involved in a range
of popular, low-key publications, must have drawn a substantial
proportion of their total income from the success of the weekly
journals, which carried their names into the farthest corners of
England. Their results were based on a prompt identification of
an area of the market not yet exploited by established members
of the trade. During the first forty years of the century a large
number of journeymen printers, hack authors and others struggled

to follow a similar path. While the first rank of entrepreneurs
moved into the provinces to open up virgin territory, those in the
second decade of the century remained in London and set up
periodicals aimed at a level of readership beneath the notice of
their more substantial colleagues. By 1725 it was claimed that at
least five London printers were supporting themselves and a
circle of commercial dependants including the makers of low-
grade paper, on the strength of their $\frac{1}{2}$d publications.[27] This
motley group are the archetypal entrepreneurs of the early
eighteenth century. William Heathcote, poised in the indeterminate
position between journeyman and master printer, was apparently
first in the field. At the age of about sixty and having lost his nose
after contracting a dose of the clap during the French wars, he
began in 1717 to publish his Original London Post. According to
his early commercial rival George Parker, who threw in these
biographical details, his paper was suppressed by the Stamp Office
after three months and Heathcote was forced to sink back to the
work of a journeyman printer again. However, in spite of his
personal and professional difficulties Heathcote bounced back.
His paper was re-established and became the main prop for the
business in Baldwins Gardens where he, and subsequently his
daughter, ran a printing office and sold stationery, forms and
patent medicine. At this level, successful production of a periodical
could be the principal means of sustaining an independent position
within the trade, obscurity being one defence against restrictive
practice from above.

   Cut-price newspapers, therefore, provided the basis for the

careers of a number of low-key but mobile London printers whose
activity, in time, did a good deal to develop new areas of the
market. The possibilities open to an entrepreneur, working outside the conventional range of book trade interests, were extensive.
The sheer scale of cut-price newspaper output, amounting, by the
mid-1720s, to perhaps a quarter of a million copies per annum,
was enough to attract the notice of a new generation of book trade
speculators.[29] However, while Heathcote, Parker, Read and their
competitors are identifiable as traditional members of the printing
trade, some of the new men entering this field are less easy to
define in terms of the standard categories. Among them Robert
Walker and William Rayner stand out as operators of a rather
different sort, separated from their predecessors and contemporaries by the scale and range of their enterprises, though sharing
in their general circumstances the familiar mixture of desperation
and flamboyance.[30] Their careers began and ended in obscure,
though not particularly humble, circumstances. Both seem to have
come from a middle-class background and Rayner, if I have
identified the right person, died in possession of a house in the
comfortable London suburb of Hammersmith as well as of a
number of newspaper shares. Although neither were booksellers
nor printers in the generally accepted sense, both ran a series of
printing offices, Rayner consecutively at Charing Cross, Southwark
and Wine Office Court in Fleet Street. Their relationship remains
unclear but there are so many points of contact that some persistent
connection seems likely. Whatever this amounted to, between them
they carved out a low-level publishing empire centred on the

periodical, which illustrates the scope which this form of publication continued to offer the individual entrepreneur.

Their earliest efforts to break into the London market seem
to have been made through the publication of a variety of pamphlets
following the popular anti-Walpole line. Material in this form lay
outside the interest of the bookseller cartels but its content fell
well within the scope of ministerial prosecution. Both Rayner and
Walker were faced with potential libel actions during the late
1720s and in 1733 Rayner was heavily fined and incarcerated in
the King's Bench Prison. Incarcerated is perhaps the wrong word
since he was able, by obtaining 'the rules', to set up a printing
office near St.George's Church in Southwark, where he pursued
his publishing interests on a considerable scale into the next
decade. By the mid-1730s both Rayner and Walker had switched to
periodical publication, producing a bewildering range of newspapers, magazines and serials and supplementing their income
from this source by an extensive trade in patent medicine.[31] The
cut-price newspaper formed only part of their output but, while
London printers working at this level seldom seem to have been
involved with more than one or two, Rayner and Walker operated
on a grand scale. Between 1734 and 1741 Rayner was debited with
the advertising duty for three weekly and four thrice-weekly
newspapers and was concerned in the production of many which fail
to appear on the official records. In this period Walker, aiming
primarily at the provincial market, was probably concerned in a
similar number produced and distributed in a way which remains
to be fully worked out.[32] In order to maximise their profits from

these sources Rayner and Walker not only diversified this output,
having a range of periodicals under way at any one time, but
showed a reasonable disregard for the rules of the game. A
proportion of their newspapers were produced in forms specifically
designed to evade payment of the stamp duty and it is possible
that both were involved in the production of the totally illegal $\frac{1}{4}$d
papers which were circulated in vast numbers during the late
1730s.[33] They pursued an equally flexible line on literary property,
filling their newspapers and serials with material owned by up-
market booksellers. However, both overstepped the line dividing
a semi-legitimate or at least tolerable use of material in a
serialisation, from straight piracy. Walker breached the Tonson
copyright by publishing Shakespeare's plays, while Rayner, who
had achieved a reputation as a 'notorious Paper Pyrate' by 1731
(publishing a spurious edition of Fielding's Welch Opera), was
involved in the obscure and complex business of duplicating
established London papers at the end of the decade.[34]

Rayner and Walker, who remain shadowy figures in spite of
their phrenetic business lives, amply illustrate the possibilities
of periodical publication at the lower end of the market. At the
same time the build-up of bookseller investment in the upper
levels of periodical output created a new set of opportunities
for the established printer. Whether acting as projector or
brought in at some later stage, the printer had a good deal to
gain by association with one of the charmed circles of 'respectable'
booksellers. Their money minimised any initial risk, while
providing a high degree of commercial stability. The status of the

printer within the framework of group ownership is usually very
difficult to pin down, as the circumstances surrounding the
establishment and conduct of individual publications remains
obscure. In practice, whether a shareholder or not, his control
of production and oversight of the initial stages of distribution
provided a strong position in case of internal dispute. Although
John Hugginson seems to have been involved in a certain amount
of bickering with at least one of the Grub Street Journal proprietors,
he continued to print the paper and by 1737 had increased his
holding from one to three shares. Similarly, three members of
the Say family continued successfully to print the Gazetteer and
General Evening Post for nearly fifty years, in spite of major
upheavals and recurrent complaints.[35] In the last resort the
printer could remove the paper altogether from the shareholders
and continue to print it on his own account, a final solution which
led to damaging splits in the London Journal, Common Sense and
the Craftsman during the 1730s.[36] While Rayner and Walker were
struggling to secure a precarious foothold at the lowest level of
periodical output (a process that must have seemed rather like
walking up a down escalator), a number of printers built up a
very substantial business on the basis of their association with
jointly-owned newspapers. Richard Nutt, for example, whose
printing office in the Old Bailey became a specialised centre for
the production of periodicals including the Daily Post, London
Evening Post, Universal Spectator and Historical Register, was
probably a shareholder in some or all of the overlapping groups
of proprietors. Nutt was a member of a well-established printing

family, but his periodical interests must have helped him along
the road to personal success. By mid-century it had become
axiomatic in the trade that a newspaper interest could provide,
not only a regular return, but the best means of obtaining other
kinds of printing work.

Advancement within the book trade by association with shareholding booksellers was paralleled by the occasional opportunities
offered by political groups, who combined to set up and direct
new periodicals. The classic case was that of Richard Francklin
who, though not a printer himself, was responsible for organising
the production of the leading anti-Walpole journal the Craftsman.
He had, it was claimed, been raised from 'very low circumstances'
to comparative affluence through his political associations and his
success story seems to have become part of the folk-lore of the
trade. In 1729 an opportunist pamphleteer, trying to persuade
Robert Walker to print one of his attacks on the administration,
was said to have proposed a meeting with a group of leading
politicians who 'would make as great a man of him as they had
done of Francklyn'.[37] Similar political influences, focused
through periodical publications, were at work in the careers of
such disparate individuals as the bookseller Samuel Buckley and
the printers William Wilkins and Samuel Richardson.

By 1740 the London book trade was divided horizontally into
strata defined, to some extent, by the overlapping activities of
printing and bookselling. The upper level was dominated by the
groups of 'respectable' booksellers and their associates, while
the lower was inhabited by a cross-section of miscellaneous

individuals most of whom were connected with the printing trade.
In the upper levels a growing sense of solidity and self-confidence
was reflected in the formal patterns of ownership and control which
by 1740, underlay all the leading London newspapers. Working in
close-knit, self-regulating groups, the booksellers, perhaps largel
through their financial holdings, were able to extend a pragmatic
control within the trade generally. One indication of this is provide
by the growing volume of complaints thrown up by individuals, who,
from the mid-1730s, were faced with a variety of restrictive
practices. The difficulties faced by non-shareholders in placing
advertisements in newspapers controlled by rivals was notorious.
Notices of a translation of Bayle's Dictionary, which impinged on
a similar group-owned property, were refused by no less than six
London papers: the Daily Courant, Daily Post, Daily Journal,
Daily Post Boy, London Evening Post and Whitehall Evening Post.[38]
A fairly typical comment on such unofficial censorship appeared
in Rayner's Penny Morning Advertiser, a cut-price paper outside
the immediate control of the booksellers - 'We are credibly
informed', it began,

> that a certain Body of Men are in a combination to oblige
> the inquisitive and studious part of mankind to purchase
> every Book they read, many before they read it by depriving
> those who lend Books of the Benefit of advertising this Design
> in the Publick News Papers: And that Mr Fancourt, who
> has opened a Universal Circulating Library, next door to
> the Royal Society House, in Crane-Court, Fleet Street,
> has been actually denied the Privilege by the Daily and
> General Advertiser, thro' the instigation of those who
> seem to be in Pain that his Subscribers should have the
> agreeable Entertainment as well as the Advantage of
> looking into such a great Variety of Subjects for so small
> an Expence. [39]

Such edgy comment on advertising policy is a commonplace of
the mid-century newspaper but bookseller action was extended well
beyond this to a general attempt to swallow up or suppress rival
periodicals. In 1740 both the Champion and the Englishman Evening
Post ran into trouble through the opposition of the bookseller
shareholders in established papers and by the mid-1740s a virtual
monopoly in the market seems to have been established.[40] The
author of the thrice-weekly National Journal claimed in 1746 that,
'As there seems to be a Combination among the Proprietors of
all the daily Papers but one, not to suffer any News-Paper to be
set up, in which they have no Concern; and as most of the
Pamphlet Shops, etc., are by Necessity or Choice become such
Slaves to them as to deny selling any Paper which has not the
good fortune to be licensed by these Demagogues; it has prevented
the first two or three Numbers of this Paper from coming to the
Hands of many Gentlemen.'[41]

As bookseller control tightened, the printers' scope for freedom
of action became much more limited. The suppression of unstamped
newspapers by the Act of 1742 was accompanied by a run-down in
the publication of all cheap periodicals. The reasons for this are
obscure and it is one of the curiosities of the 1740s that no printer
attempted to develop the penny newspaper along the lines of Rayner's
Morning Advertiser. It seems possible that the booksellers were
able, at this stage, to exert enough pressure to prevent such a
challenge to their own holdings. With this potential prop to
independence removed, success, if not survival, in the printing
trade became more dependent on a link with the structure of joint

ownership and the goodwill of the booksellers. Under the heading
'Printers' in Mortimers' Universal Directory for 1763 a note is
provided that '...in general they are employed by the Booksellers;
but their Offices are open for the reception of all proper Manuscripts from private Gentlemen; and they also undertake the
printing of Handbills, Shop-bills, Catalogues, etc.'. A statement
which perhaps suggests the limitations under which most members
of the trade were placed.

Paradoxically, the original structures of self-defence, the
'Congers', had virtually disappeared by the middle of the century.
Blagden places some emphasis on personality and the removal,
by death, of the 'keen individuals' who had brought them into being. [4]
This may be so. At the same time their decline may have been
accelerated by the sheer complexity of share dealing, in which no
single set of individuals could readily identify a common interest.
The confusion of holdings in mid-century appeared quite extra-
ordinary to an outsider. Mortimer again: 'On applying to the
Booksellers for a list of the several Capital Works printed for
each, agreeable to my first plan, I found that the property of the
principal Copies was divided into so many Shares, and changed
hands so often, that it would be impossible to ascertain with any
accuracy, to whom they belonged; I was therefore obliged to drop
this part of my design, lest it should be productive of litigation,
instead of utility.' It may also be that the development of the
circles of booksellers holding shares in a range of London
periodicals, provided an effective alternative and that the overlapping fall of one system of organisation and the rise of another

is not entirely coincidental.

To a great extent the mid-century stability of the book trade
was the product of internal manoeuvres. However, the bookseller
establishment was, so to speak, protected on the flank by its
political counterpart. Again the lines of interest meet in the
periodical. As I mentioned earlier, the Stamp Act of 1712 was
very much in accord with the thinking of the established members
of the trade. Nonetheless, it was the failure of this legislation to
deal with the periodical press and the subsequent inability of the
tax officials to establish a reasonable level of enforcement, that
allowed the lower levels of the trade to develop their periodical
output as they did. Lobbying by the proprietors of the legitimately-
stamped papers was followed by remedial legislation in 1725 and,
more importantly, in 1742 when the entire stratum of unstamped
papers was wiped out.[43] This represented a considerable victory
for the 'respectable' trade; the stamp laws, consistently enforced,
prevented the emergence of a new challenge from below. The
threat of political prosecution also provided its own oblique
support for the booksellers. One of the means by which a projector
could hope to maintain a new full-price paper on sales alone was
through the publication of racy political comment for which demand
was always brisk. Doctor Gaylord based his Loyal Observator
Reviv'd, in 1723, on this prospect and in the late 1730s Dennis de
Gettogan attempted to salvage his under-financed Alchymist
through an injection of extremist politics.[44] Both fell victim to a
swift and effective prosecution and though legal action proved
inadequate for dealing with such well-organised weeklies as the

Craftsman, it kept low-level entrepreneurial activity to a minimum.
The incidental support provided by politicians and the law buttressed
the booksellers and has a part in any explanation of the static and
prosaic character of much periodical output.

This paper has been focused on London which effectively,
through bookseller ownership of the major copyrights, controlled
the national trade. In the provinces booksellers, usually working
in isolation and with a limited market, had no scope for the sort
of intricate and specialised activity that characterised the business
in the capital. At the end of the century Richard Phillips, a bookseller in Leicester - a major centre of population and radical
politics, was apparently only able to develop his business through
the sale of pianos, patent medicine and canal shares.[45] Neverthe-
less, in the provinces, as in London, the periodical was an
important element in stabilising the position of the printer-
booksellers, providing the familiar advantages of regular income,
advertising and customer contact. Phillips's periodical output in
the 1780s was based on the weekly Leicester Herald and an
inflammatory almanac but, although the geographical coverage
was wider, his organisation was little further ahead in sophistic-
ation than his counterparts' at the beginning of the century.[46]

In the course of this paper I have attempted to link the
periodical with the main lines of development in the book trade.
In the period between, say 1690 and 1750, the possibilities of a
free and vigorous individualism were matched by an increasing
weight of group action. To some extent, this was polarised at
different ends of the market but in each case the periodical played

a key role. The gradual build-up by the 'respectable' booksellers
of a rather daunting control and the corresponding disappearance
of a whole range of peripheral book trade activity was virtually
complete by mid-century. Looking at the scope and variety of
periodical output in the 1730s and comparing it with that of the
1750s, one is struck by the growing uniformity in style and
content which is itself a reflection of the attitudes of the middling
sort of tradesmen under whose aegis it was produced. Bookseller
hegemony was not to survive the century. By 1800 new systems
of management and control, again embodied in the periodical,
were undermining the old structures. The eighteenth-century
newspaper and related forms have not received as much attention,
from any direction, as they deserve. There is not even a compre-
hensive list of such publications. However, as bibliographers,
historians and students of literature gradually push into the
undergrowth so the relationships which I have made a most
hesitant and awkward attempt to explore will take on a greater
degree of reality and accuracy.

Notes

1. Entry under this date in the General Evening Post proprietors'
   ledger, British Library Facs. X761 (xerox copy of the original
   in the W. S. Lewis collection, Yale University).

2. Reference to the portrait of John Nichols used on the cover of
   the Conference programme and taken from J. B. Nichols,
   Illustrations of the Literary History of the Eighteenth Century,
   viii, 1858, frontis.

3. For an analysis of the background to the event see R. Astbury
   'The Renewal of the Licensing Act in 1693 and its lapse in
   1695', Library, 5th ser. xxxiii, 3.

4. The Case of the Free Workmen-Printers, Relating to the Bill
   For Preventing the Licentiousness of the Press (1704) cf.
   Reasons humbly offer'd to the Consideration of the Honourable
   House of Commons (1712).

5. H. R. Plomer, A Dictionary of Printers and Booksellers Who
   Were at Work in England, Scotland and Ireland from 1668 to
   1725, reprint, Oxford Bibliographical Society, 1968.

6. This short-lived hiatus arose out of the proroguing of Parliament
   by Charles II and was accompanied by attempts at control by
   royal proclamation.

7. For a discussion of the character of this legislation see A.
   Downie's contribution to this volume.

8. This section is based largely on the material appearing in T.
   Belanger's Booksellers' Sales of Copyright, unpublished PhD
   thesis, Colombia University, 1970. See also his 'Booksellers'
   Trade Sales, 1718-1768', Library, 5th ser. xxx, 4, 1975.

9.Plomer, Dictionary. See also R.P. Bond 'The Pirate and the
Tatler', Library, 5th ser. xviii, 1963.

10.Cited in The Notebooks of Thomas Bennet and Henry Clements,
ed. N. Hodgson and C. Blagden, Oxford Bibliographical
Society Publication, New Series, vi, 1953 (1956), p.76.

11.Act 8 Anne c.19.

12.Checklist of materials concerned with literary copyright in
New Cambridge Bibliography of English Literature, ed. G.
Watson, ii, 1660-1800, cols. 283-90.

13.Both sets of volumes are on deposit at the British Library.
The Aaron Ward collection runs from 1718-1752 and that of
Thomas Longman from 1718-1768.

14.Public Record Office, Chancery 108/19.

15.Bodleian Library, 'Gentleman's Ledger B.', Mss. Eng. Misc.
c.296.

16.An attempt to avoid some degree of commercial dependence
probably underlay the establishment of a series of London
agencies for provincial papers from the late 1730s. M. Harris,
The London Newspaper Press, 1725-1746, unpublished PhD
thesis, London University, 1973, p.75.

17.M. Harris, 'The Management of the London Newspaper Press
During the Eighteenth Century', Publishing History, iv, 1978,
p.96.

18.The Daily Journal supported the administration while the Daily
Post favoured the opposition and it seems likely that all the
proprietors agreed, at least tacitly, with the political stance of
their papers.

19. This has been reprinted in full in 'The Minute Book Of The Partners In The Grub Street Journal', Publishing History, iv, 1978, pp. 49-94.

20. The higher figure is an estimate based on a view of advertising content and a great deal of oblique comment. It could only apply to a daily paper and would possibly include some proprietors who held a single share in common.

21. Belanger, Booksellers' Sales, p. 21.

22. Harris, Management, pp. 97-98, and 'The Structure, Ownership and Control of the Press, 1620-1780', Newspaper History, ed. G. Boyce, J. Curran and P. Wright, 1978.

23. Both the Grub Street Journal and General Evening Post ledgers reflect a very high degree of proprietor intervention.

24. For the position of this paper within the insurance business see P. G. M. Dickson, The Sun Insurance Office, 1960.

25. The movement of meetings between the taverns and coffee houses in the Temple Bar area, as well as the amounts to be laid out in food and drink, form the subject of regular entries in the proprietors' ledgers.

26. Harris, Management, p. 99.

27. 'Reasons humbly offer'd to the Parliament on behalf of several Persons concern'd in Paper making', n.d., Parkers London News, 988, Wednesday, 17 March 1725.

28. This and the following remarks are based on a piece of rambling polemic published in Parkers London News, 1003, Wednesday, 21 April 1725.

29. The suggested total is extrapolated from the 'Reasons', n. 27

and from estimates published in the press during the next
decade.

30.I have attempted to put together the outline of William Rayner's
career in 'London Printers and Newspaper Production During
the First Half of the Eighteenth Century', Printing Historical
Society Journal, pp. 42-50. For material on Robert Walker see
R. M. Wiles, Serial Publication in England Before 1750,
Cambridge, 1957.

31.The link between the low-level book trade and the sale of
patent medicine needs further investigation in the context of
the trading community at large.

32.The range of his activity is suggested in an advertisement for
Daffy's Elixir published in his London and Country Journal,
79, Tuesday, 1 July 1740. Distributed by Walker it was sold
by dealers in Warwick, Birmingham, Nottingham, Leicester,
Northampton, Ipswich, Bury, Stow, Devizes, Cirencester,
Bristol, Bath, Colchester, Chelmsford, Salisbury, Chippenham
'...and by the several Persons who sells the Books and News-
Papers, printed in London by R. Walker'.

33.Harris, The London Newspaper Press, pp. 20-24.

34.Rayner was apparently involved in the production of spurious
versions of the Craftsman and the London Evening Post.

35.Harris, 'London Printers', p. 36.

36.Ibid. pp. 36-39.

37.British Library, Additional Manuscripts 36, 130 pp. 171-175,
Examination of R. Walker, 31 December 1729.

38.Wiles, Serial Publication, pp. 115-116.

39. Rayner's Penny Morning Advertiser, 1223, Wednesday, 15 December 1742.

40. Champion, 64, Thursday, 10 April 1940; Englishmans Evening Post, 32, Thursday, 13 March 1740.

41. National Journal, 4, Saturday, 29 March 1746. See also the True Patriot, 17, Tuesday, 25 February 1746.

42. The Notebooks of Thomas Bennet and Henry Clements, p. 99.

43. Act 16 George II c. 2. Harris, The London Newspaper Press, pp. 25-26.

44. Harris, 'Management', p. 98.

45. D. Temple Pattison, Radical Leicester, University Leicester, 1954, p. 67.

46. Phillips' almanac-interest figures in my forthcoming review article 'Astrology, Almanacks and Booksellers' to be published in Publishing History, viii.

The Institutionalisation of the British Book Trade to the 1890s

John Sutherland

In this paper I intend to survey a critical and quite sudden episode
in the British book trade which has had consequential effects on
the production of our national literature, and helped form its
distinctive character in the twentieth century. This episode is
the entrance on the literary scene of literary institutions and
professional trade bodies in the last two decades of the Victorian
era. The formation of the Society of Authors, the Booksellers
Association, the Publishers Association, the inauguration of the
Net Book Agreement and the establishment of the commissioned
literary agent all combined radically to transform and eventually
to consolidate a specifically British literary and book 'world'.
The main features of this world are – when compared with America,
for instance – an Orwellian 'gentleness', an orderly quality achieved
by deference to custom, trade ordinance, codes of decency. All this
is the more striking since the book trade is not in itself a 'gentleman's' business; and this governing superstructure of the British
book trade succeeded a period of the most rampant free trade.

From the outset it should be emphasised that what is outlined
here is by no means newly discovered material. What I have
attempted is quite modest; to draw together published research

and reveal a significant interlocking which has not, I think, always
been sufficiently appreciated. As will be evident, the authorities I
am principally indebted to are J. J. Barnes, Victor Bonham-Carter
and James Hepburn.

Part 1 The Publishers Association, the Booksellers Association and the NBA

Between 1852 and 1890, the British book trade enjoyed, or was
afflicted by, half a century of 'free trade'. (The full narrative of
this period is given in Barnes's Free Trade in Books). Historically
this can be seen as a particularly violent swing of a pendulum
forever at movement or, at least, straining to move. Ever since
its emergence in the eighteenth century as a distinct branch of
commerce, the book trade has been marked by the contradiction
of optimistic collaborative tendencies constantly thwarted by
indomitable competitive individualism. In the eighteenth century
the collaborative tendency took the form of ad hoc combinations
of publishers, typically mustered for single productions. There
was no general or effective cartelisation within the trade until
1829, when the Committee of London Booksellers and Publishers
came into being. ('Bookseller' at this early period was still a
relatively vague term; it had not yet crystallised into its precise
notation of 'retail merchandiser of finished print commodities').
In 1829 this Committee, which formed a quorum of the London
trade capable of imposing its will generally, met and approved a
document controlling retail prices. These came to be known as
the Booksellers' Regulations, and they penalised 'underselling'

(or competitive discounts) by sanction of general boycott. Put
bluntly, if any retailer knocked too much off the price of a book
to the general public, nobody would supply him with more books.
By 1831, 650 members of the trade operated in agreement with
these Regulations, which were not, however, generally publicised.
The Committee - not surprisingly given its authoritative role -
was dominated by the most durable and venerable of British publishing dynasties: Longmans, Blackwoods, Simpkin and Marshall
(later better known as the greatest of wholesalers). There was
inevitable resentment at the 'blacklist' aspect of the Regulations,
but any effective counteraction was held in check until the 1840s.
In this decade, as Frederick Macmillan put it, free trade became
'a fetish' and 'the blessed word competition' was installed as the
holy writ of commerce.

Resistance to the Committee's discipline significantly hardened
in the 1840s, and the crunch came in 1850. At this date the
Regulations were reaffirmed, with punitive severity. Trade tickets
were to be issued and - under pain of ticket withdrawal - no more
than 10% discount was to be given to individual purchasers, or 15%
to clubs. Counterattack was led by John Chapman, at the head of
nine publishing rebels (noteworthy were the cheap publisher Charles
Knight, fiction publishers Bradbury & Evans and Richard Bentley,
the poetry publisher Moxon, the remainderer Tegg). It is possible,
if rather fanciful, to conceive of the rebellion as somehow Oedipal;
the young, vigorous new men turning against the fathers of the
trade. Whatever its deep, sub-commercial motives, the affair
was conducted with great furore. Eventually the dispute went not

to trial, but to legal arbitration by Lord Campbell. His judgement, given in 1852, was that the Regulations were 'indefensible and contrary to the freedom which ought to prevail in commercial transaction'. (It is interesting that the philosophy of free trade had permeated to the degree that it was considered even by the most notoriously protectionist of British institutions as a self-evident natural imperative.) Any 'artificial protection', Campbell opined, was wrong. In the face of this outright denunciation Longman, the leader of the old guard, declined to reconstitute the Committee. And, as Barnes records, 'book publishing began a half century of free trade'.

What exactly did free trade mean? Up to 50% discounts and the deterioration of the bookselling network, especially its provincial periphery. Various detour systems were exploited, especially for fiction: notably magazine and part serialisation (which used non-book store outlets), and circulating libraries (these were supplied directly from the publisher and could thus circumvent the now threatened bookshop distributive link). The rise of the massively popular fiction-carrying magazine (like the Cornhill) or the leviathan lending library (like Mudie) were quite conceivably a consequence of the withered condition of the retail bookselling business between 1852 and 1900.

A heroic rolling back of the free trade tide was achieved in the 1890s, largely due to the efforts of Frederick Macmillan. In March 1890 this enterprising publisher felt the time to be 'ripe for some action'. In a letter to the Bookseller he advocated abolition of the discount system in its currently unregulated form.

At first the idea, like most new ideas in the book trade, was automatically opposed. 'You can't prevent cutting', as Hatchard's manager fatalistically put it. Macmillan persisted in the face of this inertia, and elaborated a two-category scheme: 'net' books, to be sold at the publisher's stipulated price and 'subject' books, to be sold at the bookseller's discretionary price. Macmillan put the idea into practice; his first net book was the aptly chosen Principles of Economics by Professor Alfred Marshall. The initiative was successful and Macmillan's list which contained 16 net books in 1890 had no less than 137 of the new genus in 1897.

Unlike 1829, trade roles were now differentiated with some precision. In January 1895 the Associated Booksellers of Great Britain and Ireland was formed. This took as its foundation stone a resolution in favour of the net book system. In October of the same year the publishers set up their equivalent Association, similarly dedicated to the elimination of the unlicensed discount. The Society of Authors (started in 1883, its assumption of full authority was somewhat slower) was less harmoniously aligned on the subject; not until 1900 did it co-operate in forming an axis with the other two which brought about the momentous Net Book Agreement.

At first fiction was held to be less affected by the net book system than other kinds of book, since so much of its business concerned the hugely expensive three-deckers, supplied directly from the publisher. But in June 1894, W.H. Smith and Mudie agreed to discontinue purchase of the three-deckers by joint

abnegation. This was another striking example of new trade
co-operation, and the rediscovered power of group boycott in the
1890s. The three-decker's successor, the one-volume 6s. novel,
was much more accessible to bookshop sale, and with that sale
to the provisions of the net book system.

The net book system still survives, after a famous defence in
the 1960s when - in the face of a wholesale removing of retail
price maintenance - it was agreed that 'books are different'. The
NBA has undeniably given a distinct cast to the British book trade
and its ways of doing things - especially when comparison is made
with the United States. A similar scheme was set up in America,
following its observed triumph in Britain. But it was dismantled
in 1915, with the Macey case, in which the courts determined
(like Campbell) that a system based on cartelised suppliers'
boycott was commercially unfair. In the twentieth century the
American book trade has operated with far less regulation, and
far less effective regulating bodies. This it is that largely
explains why countries with a shared language, and an interest
in the same books, should have such notably different book
trades.

Part 2   The Society of Authors, Agents and Copyright Reform
The account of the formation of the Society of Authors is given
authoritatively by Victor Bonham-Carter, in his Authors by
Profession. There were a number of precursors of the organisation,
some as early as the eighteenth century. But the first significant,
if short-lived, initiative was the 'Society of British Authors' (as

they proposed to call themselves) set up in March 1843. The
society attracted a cluster of literary notables: Thomas Campbell
took the chair at the first formal meeting, Carlyle and Bulwer-
Lytton were among the speakers. Dickens took the chair at the
second meeting, Thackeray was also present. But looking back
from his own achievement later in the century, Walter Besant
diagnosed a fatal weakness in this enterprise, namely that it
ignored the copyright and ready-money aspect of things: 'there
is one thing, and one thing only', declared Besant, 'for which
those who write books...can possibly unite - viz. their material
interest.' In only a few weeks, Dickens himself had misgivings
about the Society: 'it cried Failure trumpet-tongued in my Ears',
he wrote. The whole thing collapsed in less than a year, though
some of its momentum survived in various pressure groups for
improved copyright protection for a while longer.

A starting point for the Society of Authors is to be found on
28 September 1883, when twelve literary members of the Savile
Club met in Kensington, with Walter Besant in the chair. This
apostolic body decided on a 'Company of Authors'. By 1884 an
organisation had been set up, largely due to the energy and
determination of Besant. Tennyson was recruited as the first
President, and an impressive crew of literary stars were associated
from the beginning. As initially devised, the Society's three main
objects were (1) international copyright with the US (2) a bill for
the registration of titles (3) the maintenance of friendly relations
between authors and publishers - this to be principally achieved
by the standardisation of equable contracts. It was this last aim

which drew most fire from the rest of the trade. For all its polite
phraseology it could be seen as a declaration of war. And indeed,
Besant's unswerving motive - and a motive which he grafted
inextricably into the Society - was distrust of 'rapacious' publishers.
There was none of the cosy nestling which marked the relations of
the Booksellers and Publishers in the 1890s.

In 1884 the Society was incorporated as a company with a
capital of £1,000. Annual subscription was set at one guinea.
(Members were required to be the author of one full-length work,
at least.) There were various internal difficulties in the 1880s,
but membership rose from 68 paying members in 1884, through
372 in 1889 to 870 in 1892. In 1890 it began publication of the
Author, now like the Bookseller a main organ of the book trade.
Essentially the constitution of the Society of Authors has remained
what it was in its earliest phase.

The Society began with grand expectations of what it would
achieve. Originally Besant conceived that it might become a publishing co-operative, doing away with the distrusted publisher-
middleman. In fact, its achievements have been less dramatic
and can be summed up under three heads. The Society has always
given advice to individual members on particular problems, and
has thus made more professional (if hardly more 'friendly')
relations within the trade. The Society has acted as a disseminator
of information - particularly through the Author. And the Society
has been an effective lobby: it is probably largely coincidental
that the Chace International Copyright Act went through in America
in 1891, but certainly the Society can take credit for the gradual

dominance of the royalty payment (as opposed to the iniquitous
half-profits agreement, or risky outright sale) in the twentieth
century. And much of the gradual and laborious improvement in
copyright legislation (recent PLR reform, for instance) has come
about as a result of the patient, intelligent pressure brought to
bear by the Society of Authors.

Oddly, and for reasons which are not entirely clear to me, the
Society has never undertaken any systematic agency role for its
members. It administers literary estates, but gave up reading
authors' manuscripts very early. It has also been very cautious
on the subject of authors' agents - if not as inveterately suspicious
of the breed as it is of publishers. Perhaps the Society felt a
certain uneasiness since the professional agent was very nearly
an historical sibling. In his study of the profession, <u>The Author's
Empty Purse</u>, James Hepburn distinguishes between 'precursors'
and the 'true' literary agent: 'the man who was ready to earn a
living serving the interests of several authors among several
publishers'. The origins of the true agent are hard to trace, but
one definite starting point which Hepburn can indicate is the setting
up of A. P. Watt in 1882, a year before the Society of Authors came
into being. (Watt, incidentally, was the agent the Society came to
like best.) By the mid and late 1890s one can chart clearly the
career of a dominant agent like J. B. Pinker, an entrepreneur who
came to have Wells, Wilde, Stephen Crane, Henry James, Joseph
Conrad and Arnold Bennett on his books. Arguably the literary
agent has taken longer to establish himself on the literary scene
as governing, or ubiquitous figure. But certainly by the 1890s the

better and more successful authors would routinely use his inter-
mediary services.

Conclusion

It is convenient to think of the book trade as operating on a
plateau principle, its ways stabilised by custom, tradition, pre-
cedent – until some more or less traumatic shake-up changes
things and a new plateau is found. The years 1880–1900 would
seem to represent just such a moment of transition. Having
enjoyed decades of free trade and commercial individualism, the
book trade is – within a few years – reorganised into a controlled,
multi-institutional complex. The main institutional pillars were
(and still are) the Publishers, Booksellers and Authors' Associations
the net book regime they uphold and the legitimisation of agency
services. On these pillars the admirable achievements of the
twentieth-century British book trade have been built: economic
orderliness, ethical decency, 'everlasting boom'. After Barnes's
half-century of free trade, we have had eighty years of institutional
interventionism. Given recent events, and the increasingly evident
irrelevance of rules devised in 1900, it is hard not to expect some
new and imminent tectonic shift in the British book trade.

Select Bibliography

J.J. Barnes, Free Trade in Books: A Study of the London Book Trade Since 1800, Clarendon Press, Oxford, 1964.

V. Bonham-Carter, Authors by Profession, The Society of Authors, London, 1978.

J. Hepburn, The Author's Empty Purse and the Rise of the Literary Agent, OUP, London, 1968.

P. Hollister, The Author's Wallet, New York, 1934.

R.J.L. Kingsford, The Publishers' Association 1896-1946, Cambridge, 1970.

Sir F. Macmillan, The Net Book Agreement 1899, Glasgow, 1924

Thomas Hood: A Nineteenth-Century Author and his Relations with the Book Trade to 1835

Peter Thorogood

Part 1   The Rise and Fall of Vernor, Hood and Sharpe

Thomas Hood, the elder,[1] came from Errol, a small village on
the banks of the Tay, midway between Perth and Dundee. He was
born almost certainly about the year 1759, and, being the son of
a not very prosperous farmer, he was educated at the village
school and then apprenticed to a bookseller in Dundee. Hood was
doubtless a clever child and willing to take advantage of the
Scottish system of education, at that time more advanced in the
teaching of the 'three R's' than most English institutions of a
similar kind.[2] It must have been very clear to his friends and
relations that being apprenticed to a provincial bookseller was no
match for the ambitions and broader aspirations that filled his
thoughts. It is probable that the young man came to know, or was
introduced to, a member, or members, of the Glasite sect[3] and
was given a letter of recommendation by a member of the sect to
a fellow-Glasite named Vernor, a London bookseller. Vernor,
like many another Scotsman of his day,[4] had come to London some
years previously to seek his fortune in the book trade and had
established a flourishing business in Birchin Lane, where we next
hear of Hood in 1784, or thereabouts, when he took up a position

as Vernor's assistant, a position he filled with skill and pains-
taking application. It is not surprising that, within a few years,
Vernor had made him a partner, and thus the firm of 'Vernor and
Hood' came into being, and before long had set up a prosperous
house at 31 The Poultry, a place, not of poulterers any longer
but of booksellers and publishers. Not far away, at 22 The
Poultry, were those 'worthy booksellers' (as Boswell calls them),
Charles and Edward Dilly, with whom Hood was on friendly
terms.[5] Indeed, a Scottish acquaintance of Hood's, William
Peebles,[6] wrote to inform him that Hood would soon get a satis-
factory account of his sermons from Mr. Charles Dilly, and
presumably hoped that Hood would put in a good word with the
reviewers of the Monthly Mirror. Peebles had further asked
Hood's opinion as to the advisability of securing the copyright
of his poem The Crisis, or the Progress of Revolutionary
Principles, published in Edinburgh in 1803, by entering the work
at Stationers' Hall, and again pressing Hood to bring it to the
notice of the reviewers. There is no record of Hood's reply (nor
have I seen or heard of any of his autograph letters, though some
undoubtedly exist). When so little is known of the personal life, it
is tempting to sketch the complete portrait from the merest
detail, given to us here by a virtually unknown correspondent.
Hood seems to have been the sort of man who was quite willing
to pass on his professional knowledge and skill to deserving
authors, and Peebles seems, in his turn, to have been deeply
appreciative of Hood's kindness towards him.[7]

Another member of the Hood circle at this time was Capel

Lofft,[8] the translator of Virgil and Petrarch, who, it is thought,

introduced the young poet Henry Kirke White to the firm.[9] As a

result of the introduction, Hood agreed to publish White's

Clifton Grove...and Other Poems in 1803, but it was not a great

success, only 450 copies being sold. However, an unfavourable

review attracted the notice of Robert Southey, who at once wrote

a friendly note of encouragement to Kirke White, and subsequently,

on White's death, contributed an essay for the Life and Remains

of Henry Kirke White. Capel Lofft gave in to the more persistent

entreaties of the young Robert Bloomfield,[10] who, somewhere

about the year 1798, set down the verses that came to be known

as The Farmer's Boy, published by Hood in 1800, reprinted twice

in the same year, twice in 1801, 26,000 copies being sold in the

first three years of its publication. The success of The Farmer's

Boy encouraged Vernor and Hood to publish another of Bloomfield's

works: Rural Tales, Ballads, and Songs in 1802, and although

Charles Lamb thought Bloomfield's verse poor, Hood had only to

look at his receipts to measure its phenomenal success.

Vernor and Hood published two highly successful periodicals,

one of which was The Lady's Monthly Museum. The magazine

claimed in its sub-title to consist of 'Amusement and Instruction,

being an Assemblage of whatever could tend to please Fancy,

interest the Mind, or Exalt the Character of the British Fair',

for whom it included a 'Cabinet of Fashion' with elegant coloured

plates, poems by Robert Bloomfield and others, pen-portraits of

celebrated ladies of fashion (the Princess of Wales, the Princess

Sophia Augusta, for example), and there were archly contrived

debates on such questions as whether or not long courtships are
likely to produce happy marriages, and whether works of imagination are to be condemned as injurious to the mind of youth, all
debated by such spuriously-named characters as Mr. Younghusband,
Mr. Cavill, and Mr. Meanwell. There were recipes for calves-
head pie and ginger wine, and very pure and very long-winded
novels which always somehow seem to end with the words 'To be
continued' - in brackets! There is no doubt that such a publication
as this provided the firm with a regular source of income, thus
enabling it to survive the precarious fortunes of the publishing
world at the turn of the century.

Kirke White's 'Clifton Grove' was a fine poem of the topograph-
ical kind that undoubtedly held some interest for the publisher
Hood, who had issued two years earlier, in 1801, John Britton's
The Beauties of Wiltshire, and afterwards the first two volumes
of The Beauties of England and Wales. In 'Ode to the Great
Unknown', a humorous address to Sir Walter Scott, Hood's son
Thomas included the lines

> I like thy Antiquary. With his fit on,
>   He makes me think of Mr. Britton,
> Who has - or had - within his garden wall,
> A miniature Stone Henge, so very small
>   The sparrows find it difficult to sit on. [11]

In his Auto-biography, Britton tells us that he commenced his
career as a topographer with Vernor and Hood and 'was in almost
constant communication with Mr. Hood who was the managing
partner, and who was an active, persevering, punctilious man of
business'. This punctiliousness, this careful observance of forms

and rules, was not always as clear-cut as might have been hoped
in a publisher of the 1790s. My copy of the 1797 edition of
<u>Aphorisms and Reflections on Men, Morals and Things, translated</u>
<u>from the MSS. of J.G. Zimmerman</u>, published by Vernor and Hood,
contains a cautious 'Apropos' explaining to the reader how the
work came into the hands of the publisher. Apparently, the manuscript (written in Zimmerman's native German) was entrusted
to 'an Officer of the Mortimar Regiment' for his opinion. This
officer (obviously a 'literary' soldier), on the death of Zimmerman,
retained the manuscripts because of the impossibility of dispatching
such a valuable document, since the family lived at some considerable
distance. (We note that it was not, however, too far to send them
across the North Sea to be published in England!) The (anonymous)
editor, on behalf of the publishers, wrote as follows (the italics
are mine):

> It cannot appear illiberal to publish them; for the Family
> of the Author cannot possibly be injured by their being
> translated into English. Besides, TISSOT is said to
> possess a Copy of them, which can doubtless be obtained,
> if 'tis necessary they should appear in the vernacular
> Tongue. The Editor returned the Original, from which
> these were taken, to the Gentleman whose kindness
> obliged him, and whose Permission warranted a Licence
> of Publishing.

The note ends:

> The Officer alluded to has frequently espressed his warm
> Approbation of the Sentiments and Maxims of his deceased
> Friend; and this honourable Testimony of their Merit,
> from a Soldier of enlarged Understanding, will prove,
> 'tis to be hoped, an unerring Prognostic of the favourable
> Verdict of those Judges to whom they are now submitted.

The letter of the (copyright) law is nicely challenged by such a clever choice of words: It cannot be illiberal to publish, the author cannot possibly be injured, and in the last resort, have we not the Officer and Gentleman, whose Approbation, honourable Testimony, and, of course, his enlarged Understanding, will bring a favourable Verdict? Fortunately for Vernor and Hood, the 'Judges' took little notice, and Zimmerman's 'Family' appeared to be unaware of the existence of the English version.

The case of Beckford Esq. v. Hood, reported in The Times on Saturday, 12 May 1798, brought a degree of notoriety to the firm. It concerned the publication by Vernor and Hood of Peter Beckford's Thoughts upon Hare and Fox Hunting.[12] The first edition of 1781 was published, we are told, 'at considerable expense' and bore no name on the title page. In 1782, the author published a second edition with his name, and in 1784 a third edition also with his name. In 1796, Hood published the work with the author's name on the title-page but without the consent of the author, who, we are informed, had never disposed of his right or interest in the work to Hood or anyone else. Beckford brought an action for damages against Hood, the Court following the directive of the existing statute of Queen Anne (copyright to remain for fourteen years, and for the author's life if then living). The Times Law Report concluded:

> The COURT was clear on the fair construction of the
> statute of Anne, that an author might maintain an
> action for damages against any person who had pirated
> his work during the period mentioned in the statute,
> that is 28 years. The Court was equally clear that an

Author might maintain such an action, though his
book had not been entered at Stationers' Hall. But it
was necessary that entry should be made, if he meant
to sue for the penalties and forfeitures given by the
statute. But though a book was entered at the Hall, the
Author could only sue for those penalties during the
first 14 years, but not during the last fourteen.

Clearly, Hood was, like many publishers of his day, sailing
very close to the wind. It is impossible to tell now how deliberate
or mistaken his decision to publish was; though the first edition
of 1781 (which bore no name on the title-page) was, unhappily for
Hood, just outside the prescribed fourteen year limit, the third
edition of 1784 was not. Beckford won his case against Hood,
therefore, on the grounds that the pirated version of 1796 was
within the prohibited time of fourteen years. There is no doubt
that Hood was tempted by the popularity of Beckford's book, and
may well have been surprised by the vehemence of the author's
reaction, since the expiry date of the prohibitive clause was nearing
its time. Since Hood was, as we have seen in the words of John
Britton, a 'punctilious man of business', we may assume that he
was not in any way mistaken. On the other hand, to judge from
contemporary accounts, he was 'generous and kindly' and helpful
and considerate to deserving authors, though how deserving they
had to be is not clear. The case is an interesting one, for it shows
how very close a publisher could go to the letter of the law before
legal action was eventually taken by the offended author. Beckford
appears to have been a rather irascible and blustering fellow, but
he was justified in bringing his case before the courts. Vernor and
Hood were to be involved in a more sensational case within a few year

An incident occurred in 1806 which was to bring the firm into
a situation of some notoriety. Sir John Carr, the author of a
series of personal and egocentric accounts of his travels in France,
Holland, and northern Europe, published a work entitled The
Stranger in Ireland,[13] and shortly afterwards a small volume
appeared purporting to be Carr's notes on his Irish journey,
entitled My Pocket Book, or Hints for a Ryghte Merrie and
Conceited Tour, in 4to. to be called 'The Stranger in Ireland in
1805', by a Knight Errant, and dedicated to the paper makers.[14]
The 'Errant Knight' was outraged. Had he not been favoured with
a knighthood by the Lord Lieutenant of Ireland? Were his books
not universally admired and regularly reviewed in journals and
newspapers throughout the land? The indignant Sir John instituted
an action for damages in the Court of King's Bench against the
publishers Vernor and Hood, whom the counsel for the prosecution
described as 'very opulent booksellers, and carrying on great
trade in the metropolis'. My Pocket Book was written by Edward
Dubois, the joint editor, with Thomas Hill, of Vernor and Hood's
other successful periodical The Monthly Mirror (in which William
Peebles had wished his poem 'The Crisis' to be reviewed). The
style satirises cleverly Sir John's anecdotal manner of writing.
The case, tried before Lord Ellenborough, brought fame (and to
some extent disgrace) to Sir John, and, no doubt, more business to
the firm of Vernor and Hood. The jury, without retiring, returned
a verdict of 'Not Guilty' - an important judgement against the
Plaintiff in favour of the 'Liberty of the Press'.

About the same time (1806), the firm added a new partner,

Charles Sharpe, and thus future imprints bore the style of 'Vernor, Hood and Sharpe'. It seems that Sharpe had not the business acumen and flair of his young partner, Thomas Hood, and since Vernor, possibly through age or infirmity, took a less and less active part in the running of the firm, Hood assumed an increasingly onerous share of its day-to-day activities. There is no doubt that he was considered a man of ability, as well as of honour, in the business community in London. We have already noticed John Britton's opinion of him as 'an active, persevering, and punctilious man of business', and Hessey describes him as honest and upright.[15] Certainly, he possessed the energy and drive to transform the firm of Vernor, Hood and Sharpe into a prosperous enterprise.

Some time in the late 1790s, Hood married Elizabeth Sands, the daughter of the engraver James Sands and sister of the engraver Robert Sands. Both father and son provided illustrations for Vernor and Hood publications, many of which contained wood, copper or steel engravings of a high order. Hood included in his circle, not only the Sands family, but such fine engravers as the brothers John and Henry Le Keux, who provided many of the illustrative plates for the topographical works of John Britton and Edward Wedlake Brayley.[16]

Not far from The Poultry, in Finsbury Square, James Lackington (who, with Thomas Hood and others, was a member of the Associated Booksellers) opened his 'Temple of the Muses', a remarkable building with circular galleries and an impressive dome crammed with half a million books, and requiring dozens of (ill-paid) assistants to advise customers, pack up books and collect customers' money. It was in this 'Temple' that the young John Taylor[17] first learned something of the London book trade. He had trained with an East Retford bookseller, and like Thomas Hood himself, had come to London to seek his fortune. As with a certain celebrated folk-hero, he perhaps expected the streets of the city to be paved with gold. Lackington however did not reach very deeply into his pockets to pay his young assistants, among whom were John Taylor and James Augustus Hessey. Taylor made a request for a rise in his wages, but his employer could not see his way to increasing the 7s. 6d. per week Taylor was already receiving.[18] After only four months, Taylor resigned. Undoubtedly, he had already prepared his way, through contacts in the trade, for ten days later, towards the end of March 1804, he was taken on by Vernor and Hood at a salary of £70 per annum. We are told that he worked from 9 a.m. to 8 p.m., and on the two nights when the magazines were to be issued, until 10 or 11 p.m. Taylor tells us that he found Hood 'a generous and kindly master' and came to regard him with warmth and affection. Writing home, he said, 'I am more than ever attached to Mr. and Mrs. Hood...I can say anything to them, & feel as much at ease as with you — Mr. Hood so entirely divests himself of all care when in the midst of his Family & Friends that he is always playful, & merry — and looks more like a laughing Lad than a Man of Business...'[19]

Thomas Hood, the publisher, was one of the most important influences in the life of John Taylor, who was now twenty-two years of age and ambitious to prove himself in the trade. Encouraged by his master, whose generous and warm-hearted friendship was

a great support to his endeavours, Taylor was afforded the unique
opportunity of experiencing the widest range of publishing activity.
He had a share in the production of the successful Lady's Monthly
Museum and the equally delightful Monthly Mirror, jointly edited
by Edward Dubois and the jovial Thomas Hill, 'plump and rosy as
an abbot'.[20] Hill had originally owned the magazine, but it was
taken over by Vernor and Hood and issued by them until 1810.
Praised by Robert Southey, the Monthly Mirror enjoyed a wide
readership, with its regular feature on current drama, its interesting book reviews (a reason for William Peebles' pressing invitation
to his fellow Scotsman, Thomas Hood, to review his sermons and
poems), and articles of literary, biographical and topographical
interest - in all, over sixty pages, including poems by Bloomfield,
Kirke White and others, and James and Horace Smith's 'Horace in
London'. Taylor's energy was such that he adopted the practice of
delivering in person to the 'principal people in the trade', and saw
to it that he himself received their orders for each book published
by the firm. From Taylor's letters home we learn that Hood
explained the internal organisation of the publishing trade and
allowed him to sit in on all the transactions of the house.[21] Hood
recognised in Taylor something of his own drive and ambition,
and thought very highly of his young assistant, for soon we find him
appointed, above his other duties, as reader to the firm; when Hood
was away from town, he entrusted Taylor with the complete running
of the business. Taylor tells his father in a letter of 29 April 1804
that he had 'a Levée of Engravers, Designers, & Authors, in
imitation of my Master'. In the following month, we see him

assisting in the publication of The Farmer's Boy: 'The Farmer's
Boy is now preparing to be transmitted down to posterity with the
greatest honours a Book can possibly receive - It will be the
second Work stereotyped in England. ' This new plaster of Paris
method of casting stereotypes had been perfected only two years
previously, in 1802, and here shows the progressive spirit of the
firm, for it was a costly method of printing which could only be
offset by substantial sales. Furthermore, high sales commanded
substantial sums in copyright, with minimal payments for poor
sales.[22] Britton tells us that the publishers paid Sir John Carr
something over £2,000 for copyrights. Remarkably, Vernor and
Hood paid Robert Bloomfield the astonishing sum of £4,000 for
the copyright. 'At the very beginning of his apprenticeship, indeed,
he [Taylor] learned from both Lackington and Hood a lesson which
provincial bookselling could never have taught with such emphasis.
Publishing had to do with sales and demand, finance and economics,
as well as with literary worth and excellence. It had, indeed, to
reckon with the balance sheet as well as with beauty. '[23]

Throughout 1804 and 1805, Taylor continued to work as Hood's
chief assistant, all the time establishing himself in the publishing
community, and open to any favourable proposition that might be
presented to him.[24] Accordingly, some time in 1806, he joined
in partnership with James Augustus Hessey, whom he had met
and befriended at Lackington's 'Temple of the Muses', and
together they set up in business at 93 Fleet Street, issuing the
work of Keats, Clare, Lamb and De Quincey. Thus it was that
Taylor's remarkable apprenticeship with Thomas Hood, the

publisher, came to an end, though the friendship continued for many years, even after Hood and his growing family had moved to a larger house at 5 Lower Street, Islington[25] in 1807, when Thomas Hood, the poet, was eight years old.[26] It was this house that he affectionately recalls in his now famous poem:

> I remember, I remember,
> The house where I was born,
> The little window where the sun
> Came peeping in at morn;
> He never came a wink too soon,
> Nor brought too long a day,
> But now, I often wish the night
> Had borne my breath away! [27]

To escape from the noise and bustle of the city into the comparatively rural setting of Islington village was, for the poet, not to be born, but reborn. The 'roses, red and white', the 'lilacs where the robin built', and the 'fir trees dark and high' must have seemed to the imaginative child the attributes of paradise, with heaven never very far away. But each verse ends on a darker, brooding note which foreshadows the bitter experiences that life had yet in store for him. Hessey described the boy as 'a singular child, silent and retired, with much quiet humour and apparently delicate in health'. We have to rely with some degree of uncertainty on the Literary Reminiscences for any details we possess of the poet Hood's life at this time, but we can fairly assume that he had become quite familiar with the world of books and booksellers from the earliest years of his infancy spent in The Poultry. That first view of country life at Islington, however, was to be one of the strongest of the early influences in his poetry.

Young Hood's first schooling was gained at the hands of two
maiden ladies called Hogsflesh, whose establishment was at
Tokenhouse Yard in Moorgate. From there he was removed to a
seminary at Islington and thence, as a boarder, to the Alfred
House Academy at Camberwell, where, as he recorded,

> there seemed little chance of my ever becoming what
> Mrs. Malaprop calls "a progeny of learning"; indeed
> my education was pursued very much after the plan
> laid down by that feminine authority. I had nothing
> to do with Hebrew, or Algebra, or Simony, or
> Fluxions, or Paradoxes, or with such inflammatory
> branches; but I obtained a supercilious knowledge of
> accounts, with enough geometry to make me acquainted
> with the contagious countries... [Literary Reminiscences]

His sardonic remembrance of the school in his 'Ode on a Distant
Prospect of Clapham Academy' is expressed in mock-nostalgic
vein:

> Ah me! those old familiar bounds!
> That classic house, those classic grounds,
>   My pensive thought recalls!
> What tender urchins now confine,
> What little captives now repine,
>   Within yon irksome walls?

He remembers the grim aspect of the house with its ugly windows
in rows of ten:

> There I was birch'd! there I was bred!
> There like a little Adam fed
>   From Learning's woeful tree!
> The weary tasks I used to con!-
> The hopeless leaves I wept upon!-
>   Most fruitless leaves to me!- [28]

Some time in 1811, his brother James fell mortally ill while
on a visit to his uncle, Robert Sands. When the elder Hood heard

the news, he rushed to his son's bedside, and, remaining with
him through the last stages of consumption, contracted his son's
illness, so it is said, but whatever the cause of his own subsequent
illness, he sickened rapidly and predeceased his ailing son by
four months, dying on 20 August.

Despite the apparent prosperity of Vernor, Hood and Sharpe,
the firm did not continue long. Vernor had presumably gone to the
grave long since, and Charles Sharpe, the remaining partner, did
not share the same degree of business flair shown by his late
partners. Hood, with his Scottish shrewdness and sound business
sense, had clearly been unable to maintain the same standards of
efficiency, doubtless owing to his worsening state of health, and
Sharpe was forced to declare bankruptcy and dissolve the business.
A certified valuation on the property made on 2 April 1812 shows
the firm's assets to have been £17,320.[29] After expenses and
creditors had been paid off, Elizabeth Hood and her family found
themselves in very straightened circumstances, and James,
after a protracted illness, died on 10 December, leaving behind
a bereaved and impoverished mother, brother and four sisters to
face an uncertain future.

Part 2 Thomas Hood, the Poet, and his Relations with the Book
Trade to 1835

The appalling anxieties that beset the occupants of the house in
Islington after the death of the elder Hood can only be guessed.
It seemed very clear to Mrs. Hood that she would have to find her
remaining son a place in the City until such time as he could decide

on a suitable career for himself. Through the help of a family friend, the young Thomas Hood[30] found himself perched on a counting-house stool in a firm of importers in the Russian trade, apparently called Bell & Company, if we are to believe his sonnet on the subject,[31] though it was patently clear that his love of literature was stronger than his love of ledgers:

> Time was, I sat upon a lofty stool,
> At lofty desk, and with a clerkly pen
> Began each morning, at the stroke of ten,
> To write in Bell & Co.'s commercial school;
> In Warnford Court, a shady nook and cool,
> The favourite retreat of merchant men;
> Yet would my quill turn vagrant even then,
> And take stray dips in the Castalian pool.
> A double entry- now a flowery trope-
> Mingling poetic honey with trade wax-
> Blogg Brothers- Milton- Grote and Prescott- Pope-
> Bristles- and Hogg- Glyn and Halifax-
> Rogers- and Towgood- Hemp- the Bard of Hope-
> Barilla- Byron- Tallow- Burns- and Flax!

A weak constitution prevented Hood's remaining with the firm for long, and he was sent to study engraving with his uncle, Robert Sands, from whom he learnt the basic techniques. From there, with little improvement in his health, he was placed with John and Henry Le Keux, both of whom had, at one time, been apprenticed to James Basire, and had subsequently produced plates of true excellence for the architectural work of John Britton, Augustus Welby Pugin and John Preston Neale.[32] Within a year, Hood was producing good, even saleable, work but again his health broke, and his engraving was interrupted by a severe attack of rheumatic fever, the effects of which were to remain with him for the rest of his life. He was sent, in the autumn of 1815, to recuperate with his relatives in Dundee. After his return in 1817, he rejoined the Le Keux brothers and completed a number of engraved plates, including two for Neale's Views of Seats of Noblemen and Gentlemen.

In 1821, Elizabeth Hood died. Hood wrote to his friend, George Rollo in Dundee in October, 'I have suffered an inexpressible anguish of mind in parting from my only parent, and but for the consolations which I have had I should have sunk under it'. 'The Deathbed' defines more accurately that anguish of mind:

> Our very hopes belied our fears,
> Our fears our hopes belied-
> We thought her dying when she slept,
> And sleeping when she died! [33]

One of the most affecting letters Hood wrote at this time during July 1821 was to his father's friend and former assistant, John . Taylor, now an established publisher. Hood speaks of his unsettled state of mind, his inability to do justice to his feelings, and goes on:

Had I been ever inclined to underrate acts of Friendship,
the loss of my dear Father and the consequent tenour of
my life would have taught me their full value; and indeed
I have learned to feel the full force & worth of the least
expressions and even looks of kindness. But in justice
to my heart I must declare that without this experience
and ever since the death of my brother, I have held you
in affectionate remembrance- your kind attentions to
him in his last days would have insured my eternal
gratitude even had there been no happiness in loving
one who was his Friend, nor any in the hope that I might
inherit those mutual feelings which must have been as

delightful to him as they are now to myself...When I
tell you that your kindness contributed to soothe the
last days of my dear Mother- that she mentioned your
name amongst her last thoughts and desired me to
make to you her acknowledgements...I have seen the
end of the best of Mothers. She expired with her head
upon my arm- her eyes burning towards me with their
wonted fondness, till the Spirit which looked thro them
was called away and dragging my arm from the lifeless
weight it supported, I resigned my dear Mother for
ever...[34].

Taylor had asked Hood to dine with him some time before 23

August 1820, for on that date he wrote that Hood's talents were

good, that he had written 'several clever things in Prose & Verse'

and that his assistance might be of value in relieving him of the

drudgery of revising manuscripts.[35] Hood, writing to George

Rollo in February 1821, mentions that his poems were in the

hands of 'an intelligent bookseller, a friend of mine, but I doubt

very much if he would give me proof of his opinion...'.[36] He

seemed to echo the thoughts, at this time, of his own creation,

Ben the Fisherman, who had a sanguine heart,

> And saw the future with a boy's brave thoughts,
> No doubts, nor faint misgivings had a part
> In his bright visions... [37]

The fulfilment of Hood's hopes came sooner than he expected, and

in the most sensational circumstances.

On the night of 16 February 1821, a duel took place at Chalk

Farm between the contestants of rival magazines- John Scott,

a Scottish journalist, formerly editor of The Champion, and

recently (1819) editor of the London Magazine,[38] and Jonathan

Christie, a friend of John Gibson Lockhart of Blackwood's

<u>Magazine</u>. Scott had vehemently attacked Lockhart in the pages of the <u>London</u> and the resulting bitterness between the two men over a period of six months grew out of all proportion. Defending the honour and name of his friend Lockhart, Christie challenged Scott to a duel. Scott was mortally wounded, though he lingered eleven days before he died. The need for a new editor became urgent. The proprietors, Baldwin, Cradock and Joy, now found themselves in an awkward predicament and, in desperation, approached William Hazlitt, who declined their invitation. Some months elapsed and still no solution presented itself, the journal finally being sold to Taylor and Hessey in July 1821. Taylor had gained valuable experience with Vernor and Hood, especially in his assistance with the publication of <u>The Lady's Monthly Museum</u> and the <u>Monthly Mirror</u>. Since then, he had built up a flourishing business in partnership with Hessey, and now they could add to their lists what would have appeared to be a reasonably successful magazine. It was quite natural, therefore, that he should turn to the son of his old master. As we have seen, the idea had been in the air for some time that Taylor might employ Hood in some such position as sub-editor. Hood was now twenty-three years of age, had grown up from infancy in the publishing trade, had had some experience of the commercial world, and valuable training as an engraver.

The irascible John Scott, for all his faults, had been a brilliant editor, and in the brief period of little more than a year had created in the <u>London Magazine</u> a substantial rival to <u>Blackwood's</u> and the <u>Edinburgh Magazine</u>. Hazlitt had been his drama critic,

Lamb had contributed to its pages in the guise of 'Elia', and there were others: Horace Smith, Allan Cunningham, Charles Wentworth Dilke, John Clare and John Hamilton Reynolds. Taylor, however, had nothing of the Scott flair as an editor. He was often quarrelsome and hypersensitive to criticism. His habit of altering or 'improving' the manuscripts of his contributors without consultation did not endear him to them, and his reputation as the bowdleriser of Keats and Clare did not inspire confidence in his powers of editorship. Already by 1823, Lamb had noticed a distinct decline in the quality of the magazine, and just over a year later referred to the second number as 'trash'.[39] Taylor was at least sensible enough to face up to the inevitable decline and fall of the <u>London</u> and succeeded in persuading Henry Southern, editor of <u>The Retrospective Review</u>, to take over the running of the magazine, but even he failed to revive it, and in 1829 it was absorbed into the <u>New Monthly Magazine</u>, which, ironically, Hood was later to become editor of.

Intense friendships in the book trade characterise this period — publishers with editors, editors with authors, and authors rather more rarely with publishers; yet they fell in and out with one another with remarkable rapidity. If they hated each other, they hated with passion. Furthermore, a wide variety of cases of hurt feelings made them seem more like a race of restless amateurs (in the real sense of the word) than a body of thoroughly professional men. Hood suffered continually from hurt feelings. As we shall see, there is hardly a case in which Hood did not in some way or other fall foul of publisher or editor, leading him in the end to take a

more independent line and branch out on his own, free of the
trammels of unwise agreements rarely to be kept by one party
or other and unfavourable or imprecise contracts that could end
all too easily in protracted legal battles. It wasn't only the new
Macadamised road that passed through Waterloo Place,

> Making division, the Muse fears and guesses,
> 'Twixt Mr. Rivington's and Mr. Hessey's,

as John Hamilton Reynolds wrote in his 'Ode to Mr M'Adam'.[40]
There were other kinds of division brought about by exploitation,
mercenary attitudes, petty jealousies, and manifold instances of
publishing malpractice. Even the close collaboration of Taylor
and Hessey was seen by Taylor in a strangely uncomfortable light,
when, in 1826, he wrote to Hessey, 'The Loss of the London
Magazine cut the String that tied us together, then I found that
what was called Friendship was nothing but Self-Interest'.[41]

In spite of the precariousness of his situation, Thomas Hood
gained valuable experience in the editorial field which would place
him in a position of confidence when he came to publish his Comic
Annuals, and he was able to establish himself as an author by
publishing some thirty or so pieces of his own, including as early
as November 1821, his 'Ode to Dr. Kitchiner'[42] and 'Faithless
Sally Brown' in March 1822, ending with the well-known lines on
the fate of her lover, Ben the carpenter:

> His death, which happen'd in his berth,
>   At forty-odd befell:
> They went and told the sexton, and
>   The sexton toll'd the bell. [43]

Hood's last contribution to the London was in June 1823,[44]

though, as far as he was concerned, it was not quite the last of
Taylor and Hessey, for we find Hood writing to James Montgomery
on 27 September 1823 asking for a contribution for a work to be
entitled The Muses' Almanack: 'It is intended', wrote Hood,
describing himself as 'Editor & Partner', 'to consist of poems
by our most popular & esteemed Authors, and- to fulfil my wish-
will be a kind of National Album. '[45] In the following month, Hood
was writing to Archibald Constable asking him to approach Sir
Walter Scott on his behalf for a contribution to a work entitled
Poems by Living Authors in which 'Messrs. Taylor and Hessey
& myself are partners', but neither of these works appeared. Is
it possible that Taylor and Hessey intended to take Hood into the
firm as a junior partner? We can only speculate, but we can be
certain that Hood's long-suffering nature was severely tried by
the flagging fortunes of the firm. These two new ventures may
have been launched at Hood's suggestion but, in the end, the
necessary funds could not be found. In a letter to his sisters-in-
law from Hastings, there is an uncharacteristically vicious out-
burst:

> In coming home I killed a viper in our serpentine path
> and Mrs. Fermor says I am by that token to overcome
> an enemy. Is Taylor or Hessey dead? The reptile was
> dark and dull, his blood being sluggish from the cold;
> howbeit, he tried to bite, till I cut him in two with a
> stone. I thought of Hessey's long backbone as I did it. [46]

This is the last reference Hood makes to Taylor and Hessey in
his letters. He seems to have felt badly let down in the last months
of the London's life. Now, once more, he had to look round for

other projects. At least he had made three of his closest friends
during his brief time as sub-editor: John Hamilton Reynolds,
whose sister Jane he was to marry, Charles Lamb, and Charles
Wentworth Dilke, with whom he was to correspond as editor of
The Athenaeum.[47]

In 1825 Hood collaborated with John Hamilton Reynolds[48] on a
series of mock odes addressed to celebrities of the day, and set
to work on an elaborate frontispiece entitled The Progress of
Cant.[49]   Odes and Addresses to Great People was published
anonymously by the former publishers of the London Magazine,
Baldwin, Cradock and Joy. The book was a remarkable success
and the first edition was soon exhausted. Within a few months a
second appeared, and in 1827, a third edition. Years later, in
writing to the engraver, William Harvey (the illustrator of 'The
Dream of Eugene Aram'), regarding a woodcut for Hood's Magazine,
Hood wrote: 'Let us not haggle about terms or be Cradocky'. Does
this suggest that Hood had had some difficulty negotiating the
publication of Odes and Addresses? I have not traced any further
connections with the firm, and Hood never mentions them again.
The work ensured a considerable measure of success for Hood,
and for once he was able to enjoy something of the pleasures of
affluence. On 5 May 1825, in spite of the lack of enthusiasm on
the part of Mrs. Reynolds and her daughters, Hood was married
to Jane Reynolds and the couple settled to a new life at 2 Robert
Street, Adelphi, in a house once lived in by Robert Adam himself.[50]

Hood now turned to the firm of Lupton Relfe of Cornhill for the
publication of his next book, a collection of pieces he had written

for the London Magazine and elsewhere, entitled Whims and
Oddities, which, on its appearance in 1826, William Blackwood
praised in the pages of Blackwood's Magazine for January 1827.
The facts of the case are not straightforward, for Lupton Relfe
was not the first publisher Hood had approached. It happened
that when Charles Lamb first saw the manuscript he wrote to
Barron Field, whom Hood had known as a contributor to the
London Magaziné. Lamb asked him to write on Hood's behalf to
Byron's publisher, John Murray- an appropriate choice since
throughout his life, Hood's satirical writing was greatly influenced
by Byron- but Murray did not take up the offer. On 10 October
1826, Hood wrote to Alaric Watts, 'I saw M--- for a moment,
yesterday, which sufficed for his telling me in so many words,
that the book will not suit him. I think he might have treated me
with a little more courtesy...'[51] Yet, years later in a letter to
Dickens in May 1843, Hood refers to Murray as 'the only gentleman in the trade I have met with'.[52] Jerdan[53] was of the same
opinion, referring to Murray as 'a gentleman among publishers',
but he adds that he has 'as ready a perception of the main chance
as...the most wary and greedy curmudgeon in "the trade"'. In
spite of Murray's peremptory refusal, Lupton Relfe was clearly
justified in placing his faith in the work, since it went into several
editions in Hood's lifetime. Lupton Relfe was the publisher of
Friendship's Offering[54] and had a number of successful publications in his list, but it soon became clear to Hood that Relfe
was in no position to publish a further series of Whims and
Oddities, and so he wrote to William Blackwood 'The Second

Series of Whims and Oddities is meantime in progress, - I have
had several offers for it, but if it will be likely to suit you let me
know, & I will await your proposition. ' But Hood could have
waited forever, for the proposition never arrived and the book
was eventually published by Charles Tilt. Having so far been
rejected by two major publishers, Hood was thus forced to do
business with smaller fry, who were often ruthless money-
grubbing publishers skilled in drawing up contracts favourable
only to themselves. Relfe's financial crisis was the subject of a
letter from Hood to R. Seaton (possibly Relfe's assistant) in
March 1827:

> I am much obliged by your friendly communication- &
> honoured by the confidence you have reposed in me,
> which be assured shall never be violated. The infor-
> mation, you have been so kind as to convey to me,
> was not unexpected, - and I feel bound to tell you, that
> whatever can happen to Mr. L.R. will affect me in a
> very trifling degree, as I have disposed of the interest
> I had in the work of mine, which he publishes. The .
> obligation I owe to you on that account is not diminished,
> & I beg of you therefore to accept of my thanks, as from
> one friend to another. I have the pleasure of remembering
> your name, & shall be happy to return your civility by
> any means in my power. [55]

Some time in 1826 Charles Lamb introduced Hood to Edward
Moxon, who was then employed by Longman. Moxon became one
of Hood's greatest admirers.[56] It is possible that he was instrumental in helping Hood to achieve his greatest ambition- to
publish a collection of serious poems. In July 1827, Longman
published The Plea of the Midsummer Fairies and Other Poems.
The volume contained the beautiful 'Ode to Melancholy' in addition

to the long Shakespearean idyllic title-poem, fine sonnets 'To
Fancy' and 'Silence', 'Ruth', 'Fair Ines', 'I remember, I
remember', and the finely sustained longer poems, 'Hero and
Leander' and 'Lycus the Centaur'. Though the book showed Hood
to be capable of inspired romantic writing, it was not well received
either by critics or by Hood's more superficial pun-loving public.
A small coterie, however, thought very highly of it: Moxon wrote
a laudatory sonnet beginning 'Delightful bard!...', Hone published
an elaborate prose paraphrase of the title poem by Charles Lamb,in
'The Table Book', but in spite of the support of a literary elite,
the book failed and Tom Hood tells us in the Memorials of Thomas
Hood that his father bought up the remainder of the edition 'to
save it', said Hood, 'from the butter shops'. Neither had the
progress of the book through the press been easy. Hood wrote to
Moxon that the printers had blundered by proceeding with the
minor poems before 'Hero and Leander', and complained that he
had 'not heard from Mr. Rees, & think that people "noted" for
dilatoriness ought to be protested'. Perhaps Hood should have
realised that serious writing was not going to be profitable, for
earlier in the year he had persuaded W.H. Ainsworth[57] to
publish the two-volume National Tales (imitations of the Italian
novella in the manner of A.K. Newman's Gothic romances) which
sold only modestly and received only the mildest of critical
approval:

> I have not any grief profound,
> Or secrets to confess,
> My story would not fetch a pound
> For A.K. Newman's press... [58]

Ainsworth stayed in the publishing business for only two years and
Hood was very fortunate indeed that he happened to be looking for
promising work to publish.

In April 1827, Hood's first child died (Lamb referred to it as a
'nameless piece of babyhood', a comment which did not go down
well with the family). This tragedy and a severe recurrence of
rheumatic fever, however, did not prevent Hood from negotiating
from a sick-bed the publication of the second series of Whims and
Oddities, and energetically applying himself to a great deal of
writing at the same time. Overwork and ill-health combined in
Hood to produce some of his most passionate poetry, satirical as
well as serious. His power of mind and his indomitable creative
spirit seemed, incredibly, to arise from states of the most extreme
physical debility. After the publication of the Plea of the Midsumme
Fairies, the Monthly Review described him as a comic poet trying
to play Hamlet, and he was driven back to whimsicality and punning
humour, in which, it must be admitted, he had no peer in his own
day.

> What is a modern poet's fate?
> To write his thoughts upon a slate;-
> The Critic spits on what is done, -
> Gives it a wipe, - and all is gone. [59]

Hood was often outspoken about the trade, too. Once he had
told Marianne Reynolds of 'the ogres- who are the Booksellers-
except that they have no eye in their foreheads!'[60] He did not
have much of an opinion of the younger Thomas Longman, who
had shown himself 'deficient not only in the courtesy of a gentleman, but the common civility of a Tradesman'. The elder Longman

Hood seems to have liked. Another printer and publisher Hood quickly fell in with, and almost as quickly out with, was Robert Stephen Rintoul, a Scottish journalist,[61] editor of the Dundee Advertiser until 1825, founder of The Spectator in 1828, and editor of The Atlas for which paper Hood served as drama critic. It must be admitted that Hood's dramatic criticism was not of the highest quality, and it is not surprising that he had a disagreement with Rintoul and left the paper after only four months. Later in the year, he wrote to Alaric Watts after an attack on the Literary Souvenir,[62]

> The editor of the Sunday news-wagon is a Scotchman,
> heretofore Editor of a Dundee newspaper. To my mind
> it shows no signs of editorship, and is but a hulking
> lubber of a paper; but it serves to wrap up twice as
> many parcels as any other. It plumes itself chiefly on
> its size, as though the mere superficial extent of paper
> and print ensured the spread of intelligence... A Gog
> among newspapers, - and as wooden. [63]

In 1828 Hood embarked upon yet another new venture- the editing of a new annual entitled The Gem, for which his wife Jane, who as a girl had been friendly with Keats, gave Hood the manuscript of Keats's 'On a Picture of Leander', and Hood also decided to print Lamb's 'On an Infant Dying as Soon as Born' (a remembrance of the death of Hood's first child); there were contributions by John Clare, Moore, and Hartley Coleridge, and from his most distinguished contributor, Sir Walter Scott, who sent him 'The Death of Keeldar'.[64] On 2 June 1828, Hood wrote a brief and delightfully playful letter to Thomas Gent:[65]

The Progress of Cant, engraving by Thomas Hood, 1825

Dr. Sir

On behalf of an Annual, for which I am literary A<u>gent</u>,
I apply to T. <u>Gent</u>, for the favour of a contribution.
Be pathetic, if you like, as on the Daughter of the
Re<u>gent</u>, or jest, if you please, & be Pun-<u>gent</u>, - but,
pray be dili<u>gent</u>, and for this co<u>gent</u> reason, that time
is ur<u>gent</u>.
I am Dr. Sir
Yours truly
Thos Hood [66]

The annual appeared in October 1828 in time for the Christmas

trade and was an astounding success, all 5000 copies of the first

printing sold, and about half of the second printing. In spite of the

glittering array of contributors, the undoubted masterpiece of the

whole book was by Hood himself: 'The Dream of Eugene Aram',

which Charles Tilt published separately, with designs by William

Harvey, in 1831. A letter to Abraham Cooper, however, suggests

that all was not well between Hood and William Marshall, the

publisher of The Gem. Cooper was in charge of the artistic

arrangements:

My dear Sir
I understood- (perhaps misunderstood you)- that you would let
me know on Monday whether Mr. Marshall complied with
our arrangement. - viz that I should draw for £50 on Mr.
Marshall- say from 18 Sept. to come due on the 21st.
October. 50 from 18th. October to come due on 21 November
50 from 18 of November to fall due 21 December- the Bills
to be given to me on the whole of the M.SS. for the first
Sheet being in the printer's hands. Pray let me know at
your earliest convenience that I may proceed to complete
the work. [67]

As we trace Hood's precarious journey through the ways and

byways of the publishers' London - from Lupton Relfe in Cornhill

to Longman in Paternoster Row, from Ainsworth in Bond Street
to Charles Tilt in Fleet Street, from John Murray in Albemarle
Street to Henry Colburn in Great Marlborough Street- we can
understand that his progress was not easy. Of a sanguine dis-
position, he invariably set out in a mood of enthusiasm and trust,
which, by stages, was transformed into one of bitterness and
annoyance when he often found, to his dismay, that funds were not
forthcoming- an alternating situation of raised hopes and broken
promises.

John Hamilton Reynolds wrote to Hartley Coleridge in 1829,
describing Marshall as 'a very mean, impracticable, disagreeable
sort of personage'. [68] Regarding the loss of a letter from Sir
Walter Scott, Hood later suggested to Dilke, in November 1839,
that Marshall had misappropriated it: 'After the 'Gem' was done,
a silver cup, or something, was sent to Sir Walter, and there may
have been a letter springing out of that to me, as editor. ' In a letter
addressed to The Athenaeum some years later on 23 November
1839, Hood went so far as to insinuate in public Marshall's unlawful
retention of the letter. On 18 July 1843, William Bradbury and
Frederick Mullett Evans obtained an injunction against Marshall,
restraining him 'from transferring to the title-page of...Punch's
Steamboat Companion, the frontispiece...which is printed on the
first leaf of each number of Punch'. [69] The following day, Hood
wrote to William Bradbury expressing his approval of Bradbury's
action and referring to Marshall as 'an old Pirate- & hypocrite. He
pretended to be so pious when I edited the Gem for him & offered
an original letter of Lord Byron's unprinted- he said sooner than

have a letter of Byron's in his book, he would burn the book in his
fire. But he had no objection to filch my name afterwards for
pretended Comic Annuals. ' In spite of the success of The Gem,
Hood edited only the first of the four annual issues. He had had
more than enough of Marshall's business methods. Hartley
Coleridge wrote to his mother of the matter in 1829:

> -item, that I have received a letter from Mr. Hood's
> Brother[i. e. ; brother-in-law, John Hamilton Reynolds]
> informing me that Mr. Hood has declined the Editor-
> ship of that work- referring me for payment to Mr.
> Marshall- N. -1 Holborn Bars, the person whose name
> I was applied to for contributions to the Gem, with the
> somewhat unacceptable information that said Mr.
> Marshall is a very mean, impracticable, disagreeable
> sort of personage...Hood is going to publish a comic
> Annual. I wish his speculation may not prove a tragedy
> to himself and a farce to the rest of the world. He is
> a man of real genius, and I wish him well.

I would not like to suggest, from the examples I have chosen,
that Hood's experience of the ways of publishers was all acrimony
and hypocrisy. Being the gentle, amiable man that he was, he had
no difficulty in making friends, even among publishers and editors.
His letters toTaylor, Ackermann, Bradbury and many others,
reveal a warmth of friendship that surmounted the perils and
dangers of outrageous publishers' fortunes (or even publishers'
outrageous fortunes, for that matter). His relationship with
Charles Tilt and A. H. Baily, is a sorry tale of deceit and under-
handedness. Hood's health steadily declined and he was compelled
to work, as he so often had to from now on, in bed, suffering
pitifully from alarming attacks of breathlessness and intermittent

bouts of blood-spitting. He was faced with a desperate necessity
to maintain a regular income through his own industry and ingenuity,
and, as Hartley Coleridge, Thackeray, Dickens and Browning
affirmed, through his genius. Hood typifies Isaac D'Israeli's
account of the impoverished author:

> Authors continue poor, and booksellers become opulent,
> an extraordinary result! Booksellers are not agents for
> authors, but the proprietors of their works; so that the
> perpetual revenues of literature are solely in possession
> of the trade. Is it then wonderful that even successful
> authors are indigent? They are heirs to fortunes, but,
> by a strange singularity, they are disinherited at
> birth... [70]

Undeterred, Hood now became involved in a new project. James
Silk Buckingham,[71] founder of The Athenaeum, passed the paper over
to John Sterling, who, because its affairs were in a state of some
confusion, in turn passed it on to a small company of joint-
proprietors- Charles Wentworth Dilke[72], Allan Cunningham[73],
James Holmes (the printer), John Hamilton Reynolds and Thomas
Hood. Hood seems to have liked Holmes, for, in letters from
Germany, he several times asks to be remembered to him. By
1830, Dilke had become sole editor of the paper. In 1831, he took
the surprising decision to cut the price from 8d. to 4d. a copy.
Reynolds and Hood were dismayed, Reynolds so much so that he
wrote two letters to Dilke in a single day. In the second of these,
he expressed his opinion of the situation firmly:

> Hood and I have been calculating this afternoon, and the
> result is appalling. To lower below 6d. would, in my
> opinion, be an inadvisable course, and such a fall would
> show that our previous state was hopeless. The difference

between 6d. and 4d. would be 8£ 6s. 8d. a week in a
thousand copies. The loss per annum on 5000 would be
2,165£...We are quite against the total change in our
paper-constitution. [74]

Hood, with his inherent suspicion of anything which might involve
a cut in his own meagre income, mistakenly supported his brother-
in-law's view and they both withdrew from the paper. All his life,
Hood had battled with poverty caused principally by bad financial
deals. Now he could not afford to make another error of judgement,
and in any case, he had committed himself to Reynolds' view, and
Dilke was determined to carry his policy through to the bitter end-
except that, as it happened, the end was not bitter but sweet, for
the paper's sales went up by six times the former circulation. The
financial future of The Athenaeum was assured, which could not
be said for Hood's. However, the literary and critical support the
paper was to give him in future would be of invaluable assistance,
his most important contributions being those on copyright published
in 1837. A degree of affluence had been within his grasp and he had
refused to take the risk. This situation is in striking contrast to his
foolhardy extravagance of a few years hence, which would lead him
inexorably towards complete and utter financial ruin.

For the moment, he filled his time with work for several of the
gift-books and annuals, and prepared The Epping Hunt for the press,
with designs by George Cruikshank, engraved by Branston and
Wright. [75]

It was not long, however, before Hood's natural ebullience was
restored, and his thoughts began to turn on the idea of a series of
annuals which would consist wholly of comic material, poems and

prose, illustrated with some fifty humorous wood-engravings.

As might be expected, the printing of the first <u>Comic Annual</u>, published by Hurst Chance & Co. , did not go according to plan. The printing of the volume was placed in the hands of Bradbury and Dent (who had printed the 1829 edition of <u>Whims and Oddities</u>) and one Monday evening in the autumn of 1829, Hood was dismayed to see the poor quality of the printing of the woodcuts, and in desperation wrote to William Bradbury

> You must not proceed any further with the woodcuts-
> those I have seen are far from what I wish. - I regret
> that you did not send me a proof of them before going
> to press- the last 150 of the 'Single Blessedness',
> according to the condition will be quite useless. I have
> sent the block to the Engraver & he fears it is spoiled;-
> which is a great vexation to me as I was particular
> about it, & requested you would let me know how it
> worked. [76]

A great deal of reprinting had to be done, as we learn from a letter Hood wrote to one of his contributors, Miss A.K. Knight, a designer, informing her 'that the copy of the Comic Annual which comes with this is meant merely that she may have an early one, - a better copy being in preparation'. [77] The reprinting and consequent delays caused a financial crisis in Hood's affairs. He could not even pay his doctor's bills, for in December 1829, Hood wrote to him

> I have to acknowledge your kindness & patience with
> respect to the account which I hope very shortly to
> liquidate or greatly reduce. With a good deal of
> difficulty, belonging to these times- I have got uphill
> & acquired some little reputation:- but the effects in
> profit follow at some distance. The Comic, at least,

will bring me a handsome income which you will be
happy to hear, but the profits of the first will not
be receivable, till about the birth of the second-
thanks to the System of Book selling & Bills at 9
months which with me are most difficult of discount.
I am accordingly prest at present, - but after the
publishing acct. in February shall be in possession
of my Bills, - which I hope will be in part convertible, -
& you may rely upon it, the very first consideration
with me will be your claim on me. [78]

In spite of these difficulties, the Comic Annual for 1830 was
an unqualified critical success. Hood had dedicated it to the
Secretary of the Post Office, Sir Francis Freeling (himself a
book-collector), and had named his daughter, born on 11 September
1830, Frances Freeling in his honour. However, Bradbury broke
with Dent, and formed a partnership with Frederick Mullet Evans,
who had worked at Longman's with Moxon when Hood had published
his volume of serious poetry. Bradbury and Evans were to continue
to do work for Hood for a number of years, printing all the Comic
Annuals until 1839, as well as Hood's humorous account of his
German travels, Up the Rhine.

Hood was a perfectionist in his literary productions and sought
standards of excellence in the quality of the paper, binding and fin-
ishing , type-face, general lay-out, and, especially the fineness
of the printing in the woodcuts. He was not only a perfectionist,
he was also an illusionist, for the very standards he hoped for
were simply not attainable, in the main, from the mediocre
publishers he was constrained to employ. In some ways, we must
admire them for achieving what they did with the limited funds
they were prepared to place at Hood's disposal. And what a

frequently contentious and demanding task-master Hood invariably

turned out to be! The little gilt-edged volumes, with their plum-

coloured spines and gilt lettering, their clever display of prosaic

and poetical pleasures, interspersed with humorous wood-

engravings, had a unique charm which was the delight of every

reader from low-brow to high-brow.[79]

Hood, after the fiasco in the printing of the first Comic Annual,

broke off with his publishers, Hurst Chance & Co., and was greatly

irritated when they announced the forthcoming New Comic Annual,

misleadingly advertised together with Hood's own authentic works.

Louisa Sheridan's Comic Offering, another imitation, ran simul-

taneously with Hood's Comic Annuals until 1835. In the Preface

to the Comic Annual for 1831, Hood remonstrated with this growing

band of imitators:

> Now, I do not intend, like some votaries of freedom, to cast
> mud on the muddy, nor dirt on the dirty- but while I am
> on the hustings, I will ask the Committee of that Uncandid
> Candidate, "The New Comic", whether it was quite honest
> to canvass against me under my own colours,...Were
> there no other and fitter labels extant than those close
> parodies of mine?...In the Announcement of "The Comic
> Offering"...it is insinuated that I am an author unfit
> for female perusal:...Miss Sheridan and modesty compel
> me to declare that, many Ladies have deigned to request
> for their albums some little proof of "the versatility" or
> prosatility of my pen:- yet what says the Announcement,
> or rather Denouncement? "But shall we permit a Clown
> or Pantaloon to enter the Drawing-room or Boudoir; no,
> not even under a Hood!...

Hurst also published another rival annual, The Humourist, edited

by W.H. Ainsworth, who had, somewhat precariously, established

Hood as a writer of prose with the publication of the <u>National Tales</u>.
Hood felt decidedly betrayed when he discovered that the publisher
of his <u>Comic Annual</u> had set up in competition with annuals blatantly
identical both in content, and format. Even worse, he had actually,
by virtue of the mere printing of it, publicly condoned an opinion
that Hood's work was actually unfit for female perusal. In fact,
nothing could have been more suitable for family reading than Hood's
Comic Annuals, and, happily for him, their success was assured for
years to come, but now with the aid of yet another publisher.

In the meantime, Hood completed work on his <u>Comic Melodies</u>
which were set to music by Jonathan Blewitt in 1830, and published
by Samuel Chappell. Blewitt also set three of Hood's comic songs
in the Ballad Singer. In reply to a note from Chappell, Hood wrote
in November suggesting Chappell might call on him to discuss the
content of a former letter to Chappell in which Hood 'precisely
states the case as it stands' between Mr. Blewitt and himself,
which suggests all was not well again in the matter of contractual
terms and agreements.[80]

Hood's popularity was at last assured. Years later, Mayhew,
writing on the second-hand book trade, declared that the poems of
Hood, Shelley, Coleridge, Wordsworth, and Moore, seldom turned
up on the stalls. Now there is hardly a bookseller in the country
who has not at least one copy of Hood's poems in the ubiquitous
Moxon, Ward Lock, Chatto, and Oxford University Press editions.
I can only assume that Moxon's abundant posthumous editions of Hood's
works had not yet reached the second-hand market, and that his
readers still had an affectionate regard for his work, a regard

lamentably lacking today.[81] Yet Hood's works were even more
popular in the fifty or sixty years following his death than in his
own lifetime.

Hood now turned for the production of his next Comic Annual
to the publisher Charles Tilt. The Comic Annual for 1831 was
dedicated to the sixth Duke of Devonshire, who became Hood's
patron and was kind to him over the years, as he was to many an
artist and author. As has been patently clear in the case of Thomas
Hood, (which I have recounted with what I hope is a judicious choice
of its complexities), the gradual shift of patronage from the wealthy
patron to the bookseller/publisher did not necessarily improve the
status of the author, and Hood was fortunate to enjoy the encouragement and support of one of the most distinguished English patrons
of his time, indeed of all time.

By 1833, Hood's success reached a peak (and as we shall see,
to some extent led to his undoing). Tilt advertised for sale a new
novel, Tylney Hall (dedicated to the Duke of Devonshire) to appear
in the following January, the Comic Annuals for 1830, 1831, and
1832, Whims and Oddities in Prose and Verse (now in its fourth
edition), The Plea of the Midsummer Fairies (presumably taken
over from Longman's), The Progress of Cant (originally published
by Thomas McLean), The Epping Hunt and Comic Melodies (now
'lately published' by Clementi and Co.). Things could not have
been, had never been, and would never be better for Hood; God
was in his heaven, Tilt was in his counting-house, counting out
his money, and almost all was right with the world- except, that
is, for Tilt, whose dilatoriness (had not Hood once accused Rees

of the same fault?) in sending out copies of the <u>Comic Annual</u> for
review seems to have annoyed Hood, who had written to his
engraver friend, John Wright, to explain all he could about
William Jerdan.[82]

Jerdan's <u>Literary Gazette</u> for 15 December reviewed the book,
but only just, for Tilt had sent it very late in the week in question.
Hood asked Wright to explain to Tilt that it was the custom to
review before publication. Tilt apparently made some sort of
objection, or at least some expression of indifference on the
matter, since Hood found it necessary to write to Tilt again, for
it seems Jerdan must have had to review the book from the unbound
sheets, or at best from a proof copy. Tilt was clearly very late
for the Christmas trade, and Hood told him it was already too
late to stop the review which Dilke was to publish in <u>The Athenaeum</u>,
also on 15 December. 'I am all but done-,' Hood wrote to Tilt,
'shall be by Saturday & Bradbury's must push on night and day if
necessary- & we have nothing for it but to get out as soon as
possible after the notices.'[83]

The rift between Hood and Tilt was inevitable. In a letter to
Dilke from Germany on 17 January 1836, Hood is more explicit
about their differences:

> ...as a corroboration of my notion of Tilts villainy let
> me just mention the following. I sold 500 of my <u>first</u>
> annual (with Hurst & Chance) to America. Of the <u>second</u>
> I sold some more having been applied to <u>myself</u>, for
> some. After that for 3 years I sold none <u>Tilt</u> telling me
> there was no demand or that the Americans reprinted
> it. For the 6th annual, in Baily's hands, I have a demand
> again for 500- & amongst the letters sent out to me is

one from Philadelphia, with an offer of money for
early sheets to reprint in Knickerbocker's Magazine
of New York. It says 'you are every where admired
in the best parts of America & your puns & sayings
are extremely quoted. I think that the advent of
your annual is a matter of as much moment in this
country as that of the President's message.'
Coupling this with the late order for 500 & knowing
the Americans cannot well reprint for want of wood-
cutters, I think 'tis at least a suspicious case. [84]

In the following year, Hood would publish three letters on

copyright, Copyright and Copywrong in the pages of The Athenaeum.

The matter of author's rights became for him almost a crusade,

and his letters to Dickens (the principal crusader with support

from Thomas Noon Talfourd in the House of Commons) reveal

Hood's deep concern for what Isaac D'Israeli called 'the calamities

of authors'. To Wright, again from Germany, Hood said: 'I am

glad you like my Letter on Copyright. I have got the Athn. with

the 2nd. part- I think remembering Tilt I have let off the book-

sellers very easily.' Without doubt, Tilt displayed the less

attractive aspects of the smaller and less well-known publisher.

One of the problems that perenially faced Hood, as a freelance

author, was not, as it is today, the eminence grise of the tax

inspector peering ominously over his shoulder at the balance

sheets, but the grey spectres of grasping and unscrupulous

publishers, the inadequate copyright laws, pitifully low

royalties, and ever looming on the horizon, the grim prospect

of the Insolvent Court.

About this time Hood, largely through folie de grandeur, moved

to the extravagant surroundings of Lake House, Wanstead (the setting for Tylney Hall), with its fading murals, classical portico, its lake, set in acres of land infested with rabbits. Tylney Hall, Hood's first novel, was published, not as announced, by Tilt, but by A.H. Baily, who also took over the Comic Annuals from 1834. This was a year Hood was never to forget or recover from. In December, Charles Lamb, one of Hood's oldest and closest friends, had a serious fall in Church Street, Edmonton and, two days after Christmas, died of erysipelas. Just as Lamb had been deeply shocked by the death of Coleridge five months before, so Hood suffered inconsolable grief at the loss. In Islington days, they had met at least three times a week, and had kept closely in touch over the years.[85] Writing to Thomas Colley Grattan in 1837, and lending him a copy of Lamb's Letters, he said 'Lamb was an odd man and a shy one. It was necessary to know him to understand him, - to understand him, to like him, - but then, you loved him.'[86]

The fatal year of 1835 began auspiciously enough with the birth of a son to Thomas and Jane, christened Tom.[87] But before the year was out, Hood was to have experienced a flurry of misfortunes that would all but crush his spirit. It was to be the worst year of his life, when he was forced by the most distressing of circumstances to face up to the hardest and cruellest realities. First, the difficult birth of Tom Hood brought Jane to the very edge of death. For weeks she lay gravely ill at Lake House, Hood often sitting up all night with her and holding her hand to comfort her. The Reynolds sisters Marianne and Charlotte, arrived from Norfolk to find the family living in conditions nothing short of poverty. They berated

Hood for allowing their beloved sister and her new-born child to suff
such degradation, and threatened to remove them to more salubrious
surroundings until such time as Hood could afford to keep them in
some degree of comfort. Hood resisted these entreaties and threats,
believing all the time that things would improve. Fortunately, Fanny
caught the measles and the intransigent in-laws were driven from
the house, leaving Hood to face an absolutely desperate financial
crisis. He had no-one to turn to. It seems that he was involved in
some way with Branston and Wright, a contract perhaps, or a
mutual commitment of some kind, and when the firm went bankrupt
in 1833, Hood had clearly found it difficult to meet the financial
demands made on his meagre resources. Tom Hood, in his
Memorials of Thomas Hood mentions a 'very heavy loss'; Walter
Jerrold refers to 'the failure of a publishing firm'; Jane Hood in
some notes on Hood's publishing career claims that his money
troubles began 'about 1833 or 4 caused by the failure of Mr. Wright';
Frederick Oldfield Ward in the unpublished account of Hood's
hardships, 'The Case of Mr. Hood', which was submitted to Sir
Robert Peel in 1844, in connection with an appeal on Hood's
behalf for a Civil List pension, wrote: 'He labours under pecuniary
embarrassments occasioned not by any imprudence or extravagance
on his part, nor even by any circumstances which he could foresee
or control, but by the bankruptcy of Messrs. Wright and Branston
in 1833.'[88] Unlike many of the other business associations Hood
formed in his life, he did not break off his friendship with Branston
and Wright, and he seems to have been a loyal support to them
in their time of crisis. In fact, he went so far as to allow Branston

to set up a work-room over the stable at Lake House, and after Hood left the house, Branston moved in, to be the last tenant of the house before its demolition.

Hood's domestic aspirations tended to attract him towards the more fashionable quarters of London: The Adelphi, St. John's Wood, and a country estate at Wanstead- encouraging him to pay over the top for the privilege of being able to show off his homes to his friends and acquaintances, and frequently to impress his business associates. He was also extremely, and sometimes extravagantly, hospitable, and, it must be said, played the host in a most engaging and delightful manner that endeared him to all who had the opportunity of an invitation. This generosity was one of the bones of contention with the Reynolds family, that he chose to live always beyond his means without the necessary financial security to back it. Charles MacFarlane, in his Reminiscences of a Literary Life has given a highly-coloured account of Hood's life at Winchmore Hill, and his subsequent removal to Lake House:

> Hood had no head for business, no system, no management, and he spent money as fast as he got it. For some time, he occupied a pleasant little cottage in the right pleasant valley of Winchmore Hill...It was certainly house enough for him; but Tommy did not think so, and all of a sudden he was invaded by the insane fancy that he could save expenses and even make money by farming- he who scarcely knew grass-seed from gunpowder. So after a lucky hit with some book or other, he went away and took a large house on the edge of Epping Forest, quite a mansion and manor-house, with extensive gardens and about eighty acres of land attached. As the house was so roomy, he could give his friends beds, and as a general rule those who went to dine stayed all night, and a part of the next day.

The house was seldom devoid of guests, the distance
was so convenient, and Tommy's cockney friends liked
to breathe country air, and took up quite a romantic
passion for the Forest. His household expenses were
treble what they had been in the snug, pretty little
cottage at Winchmore Hill: and then the farm ran
away with a world of money. It may be imagined how a
thorough cockney, one born and bred in the Poultry,
Cheapside, a poet and punster, would farm! What
with his hospitalities and what with his agricultural
expenditure, he became seriously embarrassed. [89]

Such a description has something of the comical about it, yet

we cannot deny that Hood's intentions were largely praiseworthy

ones: his natural kindness and generosity, for example, was not

as misdirected as MacFarlane suggests, yet there is some element

of truth in the suggestion that Hood's tendency towards a certain

'grandiose folly' at this time had brought him to the point of

bankruptcy. He had, as it turned out, unwisely placed himself

firmly in the clutches of a new publisher, A.H. Baily. In 'Stanzas

on Coming of Age'[90] Hood looked to the freedom that money could

give:

> I'm free to give my I O U,
> Sign, draw, accept as majors do;
> And free to lose my freedom too
> For want of due assets.

The prospect of bankruptcy is horrendous at any time, but in

Hood's day especially so. In the eighteen months following December

1825, no less than 101,000 writs of arrest were issued for debts

unpaid. In the year ending 1830, 7114 persons were sent to the

Debtors' Prison, in London alone. Hood could not, alas, benefit

from the favourable and more humane changes that would come

about only a few years hence. Ironically, his publisher, A.H.
Baily, with whom he was to suffer more deceit than even Tilt had
displayed, announced for publication Scenes and Stories by a
Clergyman in Debt, purporting to have been written during his
confinement in the Debtors' Prison, and giving factual accounts
of usurers, sheriff's officers, attorneys, money-lenders 'and
their tribe', and gave instances of the incarceration of distressed
tradesmen, fallen roués, practised swindlers, shipwrecked
dramatists, and, need it be mentioned, poor authors. The Literary
Gazette reviewed it:

> The avowed object of this work is to demonstrate the
> evil of imprisonment for debt; and it is evidently the
> production of one who has tasted the bitterness of that
> condition, and seen how ruinously the practice wrought
> both for the honest debtor and merciless creditor. The
> subject is one of great national interest, and as far as
> this exposition goes, we trust it will increase the
> attention which humanity and policy have already
> directed to the application of a remedy.

The Times reviewer wrote:

> It undertakes to give an account of the interior of the prison,
> of the economy of sponging-houses, of the extortions
> of sheriff's officers, of the immorality of the prisoners,
> of the iniquity of the law of arrest for debt, and the
> abominations of the Insolvent Court.

I quote these two reviews as a testimony of the horrors that awaited
the bankrupt before legislation was introduced to protect the debtor
from such indignities. If only Hood had read the book! Perhaps
he might just have been deterred from his reckless extravagance.
Yet one doubts it, for his natural gregariousness and open-hearted
friendship would not allow any such constraint. He succumbed with

as much dignity as he could muster. After the final collapse of his interests, he wrote to Dilke 'The struggle to maintain caste is indeed a bitter one and after all I fear we must say, "le jeu ne vaut pas la chandelle"'.[91]

Hood now faced the worst decision of his entire life: to stay and endure the suffering, shame and privation of the Debtors' Prison, or go into self-imposed exile. It is to his credit that he bravely chose the latter, but not without the most agonising heartache. He had, in his life, made the closest of friendships, and now, two friends came forward to manage his affairs in his long absence abroad- Charles Wentworth Dilke and John Wright. Leaving his affairs in their capable hands, he placed his wife and children in the care of Dr. William Elliot (who had attended Jane during her long illness at Lake House). Thus determined, in the words of the Memorials, he 'voluntarily expatriated himself'. Some years before in the Plea of the Midsummer Fairies volume, he had written a poem entitled 'The Exile'; he could not have realised how much meaning his youthful words would have in the future, still less that they should ever apply to himself:

> The swallow with summer
>   Will wing o'er the seas,
> The wind that I sigh to
>   Will visit thy trees,
> The ship that it hastens
>   Thy ports will contain,
> But me-- I must never
>   See England again!
>
> There's many that weep there
>   But one weeps alone,

> For the tears that are falling
>   So far from her own;
> So far from thy own, love,
>   We know not our pain;
> If death is between us,
>   Or only the main.
>
> When the white cloud reclines
>   On the verge of the sea,
> I fancy the white cliffs,
>   ; And dream upon thee;
> But the cloud spreads its wings
>   To the blue heav'n and flies.
> We never shall meet, love,
>   Except in the skies! [92]

One chapter in the life of Thomas Hood was ended. The next was to be equally fraught with problems, and is, in many ways, an interesting story for the student of publishing history.

Aristotle tells us that tragedy must be of a certain magnitude: 'The change of fortune', he wrote, [93]

'must not be the spectacle of a virtuous man brought from prosperity to adversity, for this moves neither pity nor fear; it merely shocks. Nor, again, that of a bad man passing from adversity to prosperity, for nothing can be more alien to the spirit of tragedy;... Nor can the downfall of the utter villain be exhibited. A plot of this kind would, doubtless, satisfy the moral sense, but it would inspire neither pity nor fear; for pity is aroused by unmerited misfortune, fear by the misfortune of a man like ourselves. Such an event, therefore, will neither be painful nor terrible. There remains, then, the character between the two extremes-that of a man who is not eminently good or just, yet whose misfortune is brought about, not by vice or depravity, but by some error or frailty.' [94]

Hood's life-story has something of the elements of such a tragedy.

There are certainly the villains who rose to prosperity, and some
of them contributed to his downfall. There is a virtuous protagonist,
brought to adversity; there is a deal of misfortune- so much of it
that, taking the view that truth may after all be stranger than fiction,
the verisimilitude of a play based on the incidents I have described
would stretch the bounds of credibility. Above all, there is the
error and the frailty. Have we not, therefore, the elements of a
kind of personal tragedy? The story of a man forcibly separated
from wife and children to live in exile in a foreign land is tragic
enough. It happens all too often. Hood's struggle to overcome
bouts of ill-health and to maintain in the face of adversity what
he called his 'Cheerful Philosophy' became almost a legend in his
lifetime. Thackeray wrote of it, Dickens wrote of it, the ordinary
working man spoke of it. But the law would not listen.

> I've heard about some happy Isle,
> Where ev'ry man is free,
> And none can lie in bonds for life
> For want of L.S.D. [95]

For Hood, as yet, that 'happy isle' was not to be England.

We do not have to imagine the turmoil of mind and spirit that
was to assail Thomas Hood during that fateful crossing to
Rotterdam, for it is written down for us in his letters home. We
do not have to know much about publishing history to understand
the difficulties he had to contend with, over a period of five years
in exile, in keeping his works before an ever-increasing public,
both in England and America. Admittedly, John Wright was in
London to cope with immediate problems and to see the proofs
through the press. But there had to be constant communication;

posts were erratic, vital letters were lost or misdirected,
supplies of paper and pens had to be dispatched, consignments
of woodblocks for his comic engravings, copies of the latest
papers and journals, and there was always the ever-present threat
of the Insolvent Court hanging over him should he return to England.
Meanwhile, Baily was publishing the <u>Comic Annuals</u> and keeping
the books according to the book of Baily!

To those admirers of 'Faithless Sally Brown' and other comical
pieces, the portrait of Hood depicted in the events I have described
may be hardly recognisable. Yet the man and the work are of a
piece, for the face of the clown is but a mask also. If he had been
offered a second chance to return to earth for another crack at life—
and remembering the world to be partly inhabited by Tilts and
Bailys, I fancy he would have refused. The game, in Montaigne's
words, was not worth the candle. But his love of the world, of
family and friends, the pleasures of poetry, and his determination
to meet all challenges head on, would have encouraged him to
decide otherwise. One other of life's attributes, above all else,
one which his publishers had ruthlessly exploited, and refused in
their own interests, fully to comprehend, was Hood's profound
and abiding belief, against all the evidence to the contrary, in the
dignity and pride of authorship.

Notes

Author's note: My purpose in this paper is to show how Thomas
Hood, the author of The Dream of Eugene Aram and The Song of
the Shirt was born into and grew up in the book trade, and how,
by dint of the calamities of authors and the malpractice of booksellers, he was compelled to go into exile in 1835. Part 1
traces the history of his father's publishing house and gives
something of the background to Hood's early family and professional
life. Part 2 gives an account of his relationships with his
publishers up to 1835.

1. In Part 1 references to 'Thomas Hood' and 'Hood' refer to
   the elder Thomas Hood unless otherwise indicated.

   Confusion has arisen in the correct nomenclature of the three
   generations of Thomas Hoods . Principally, there is Thomas
   Hood, the poet, (designated by some bibliographies as 'Thomas
   Hood, the elder'); his father, Thomas Hood, the elder by right,
   is rarely included in biographical dictionaries; his son, Tom
   Hood, was christened so, but does not help by calling himself
   (presumably in honour of his father) 'Thomas Hood' on the title-
   pages of his books. Thomas Hood, the poet, is frequently
   referred to as 'Tom' by his admiring and affectionate contemporaries.

2. The Nonconformist insistence on bible reading brought about a
   higher level of literacy in the Scottish schools.

3. John Glas, minister of the Church of Scotland, published his
   Testimony of the King of Martyrs concerning His Kingdom

(based on the controversial John xviii:36) 1727, in which he
opposed the national churches, and described the doctrines,
ordinances and discipline of the Christian Church as given in
the New Testament. For this he was dismissed from his
ministry and founded the Glasite Sect, which flourished in and
around Dundee. Similar churches were established on primitive
models in London by his son-in-law, Robert Sandeman. Vernor
was almost certainly a member of the London branch of the
sect, and Hood, the elder, may have attended its meetings too.
This background of nonconformity provided Thomas Hood, the
poet, with an entirely independent turn of mind on questions of
religion.

4. I am not aware of any existing study of the influence of the
Scottish book trade on the London book trade. See R.D. Altick,
The English Common Reader, 1800-1900, Chicago, 1957, pp.9-10.

5. John Stow mentions in his Survey of London, 1598, that the
poulterers began to desert their traditional place of business.
No doubt because of The Poultry's reputation as a thriving
commercial community, publishers and booksellers seized the
opportunity to set up in business there, issuing works by Chaucer
and Skelton among others. After the Great Fire of 1666, businesses
were re-established. In 1678, Nathaniel Ponder published the
first edition of Bunyan's Pilgrim's Progress there. Almost a
century later, in 1759, the year of Hood the elder's birth,
Charles and Edward Dilly (whom Boswell mentions many times
in his Life of Johnson) set up in business at 22 The Poultry,
where the 'hospitable and well-covered table', Boswell tells us,

was attended by 'a greater number of literary men than at any

other'. Charles Dilly was Master of the Stationers' Company in 18

6.William Peebles (1753-1826), son of a draper of Inchture, where

for a short time he taught at the parish school. Educated at

Edinburgh University. Ordained 1778. Married Jean Home,

1781. A number of his children pre-deceased him, including

Margret (died 1788, aged four) and Anne (died 1788, aged three)

who are undoubtedly the children referred to in the letter to

Hood. For information concerning William Peebles I am grate-

ful to the Revd. Lawrence Linton of Brighton, and to Professor

Allan Galloway of Glasgow University. Peebles published a

number of works including Sermons on Various Subjects,

Edinburgh, 1794. See Fasti Ecclesiae Scoticanae, Edinburgh,

1920.

7.   'It gives me sensible pleasure to hear you and your family

are well; am sorry that any of your Children should have

been taken away from you; I can well sympathise with you,

as I have also drunk of this bitter cup, having lost two

of my children; I have still eight alive, several of whom

are from home, in different branches of business. You

have indeed been a great Stranger to Scotland, and I am

persuaded that a visit now after so long an absence would

not yield you very great pleasure.

When you can find any leisure time, I shall be happy

to hear from you. I could give you some account of some

Inchture friends, but I suppose you can scarce remember them.

From an autograph letter in the author's Thomas Hood Collection.

8. Capel Lofft (1751-1824), barrister at Lincoln's Inn, 1775. Settled in Turin in 1822. Published translations of Virgil and Petrarch, 1775-1814. His son, Capel Lofft (1806-1873) was a classical scholar.

9. Henry Kirke White (1766-1823), son of a Nottinghamshire butcher, eventually obtained a sizarship at St. John's College, Cambridge, where overwork brought about his early death.

10. Robert Bloomfield (1771-1823) worked as a shoemaker under his brother George in London. Manufactured Aeolian harps. Embarked unsuccessfully in the book trade.

11. John Britton (1771-1857), Antiquary. Before his time, popular topography was not widely known and he originated an entirely new kind of literary work. Published fourteen volumes of Cathedral Antiquities in England, 1814-35. His Autobiography was published in 1850, with engravings by Hood's brother-in-law, Robert Sands and others by Le Keux, both of whom taught the younger Thomas the art of engraving.

12. Peter Beckford (1740-1811), Master of Foxhounds, scholar and author of books on hunting. This account of the case was taken from The Times, 12 May 1798 (in the author's Thomas Hood Collection).

13. Sir John Carr (1772-1832), traveller and barrister of the Middle Temple, travelled mainly for reasons of health.

14. For an account of this work, see The Annual Review, vii, 1808. An account of the trial was published, with several letters from the Earl of Mountnorris, Sir Richard Phillips and Edward Dubois.

15. See A. Elliot, Hood in Scotland, Dundee, 1885, pp. 18-19.

16. Edward Wedlake Brayley (1773-1854), topographer and archaeologist, associated with John Britton in several publications including The Beauties of England and Wales. Hood also published works by Brayley and William Herbert.

17. John Taylor (1781-1864), publisher of Keats. Proprietor of the London Magazine (1821-4). Author of Identity of Junius... established, 1816 (see Sir Phillip Francis in DNB). Also associated with Charles Wentworth Dilke (see note 47).

18. T. Chilcott, A Publisher and his Circle: The Life and Work of John Taylor, Keats Publisher, London, 1972, p. 8.

19. Ibid, p. 9.

20. C. A. Prance, The Laughing Philosopher, London, 1976, p. 54.

21. Chilcott had access to the Bakewell Collection of autograph letters, owned by a descendant of John Taylor's brother James, a Mr. R. W. Cockerton of Bakewell.

22. see Altick, The English Common Reader, p. 262.

23. Chilcott, A Publisher and his Circle, p. 11.

24. Ibid. (Bakewell MSS, 28 August 1804).

25. Now the Essex Road.

26. Thomas Hood (1799-1845). Hood was born on 23 May 1799 at 31 The Poultry. A plaque on the wall of the Midland Bank now standing on the site commemorates the event.

27. W. Jerrold ed., The Collected Works of Thomas Hood, Oxford, 1906, p. 185.

28. Ibid. p. 411. The director of the Academy was Nicholas Wanostrooht (1745-1812), a Belgian teacher of French, who came to England some time before 1780, and by 1795, had

opened his private school in Camberwell. He published a
French grammar, 1780 and a vocabulary, 1783.

29.The original document is in the Bristol Public Library.

30.In Part 2 references to 'Thomas Hood' and 'Hood' refer to
Thomas Hood, the poet unless otherwise stated (see note 1).

31.Jerrold, The Collected Poetical Works, p.303. 'The Bard of
Hope' was a name of Thomas Campbell, author of The Pleasures
of Hope, published in the year of Hood's birth, 1799.

32.Henry Le Keux (1787-1868) engraved for works by John Britton
among others, and also for the fashionable Annual (1820-40).
John Le Keux (1783-1846) engraved plates for John Britton,
Augustus Welby Pugin and John Preston Neale.
John Preston Neale (1780-1847), architectural draughtsman,
executed drawings with a pen and tinted them with water-colours.

33.Jerrold, The Collected Poetical Works, p.444. For the letter
see P.F. Morgan, The Letters of Thomas Hood, Edinburgh,
1973, p.29.

34.Morgan, The Letters of Thomas Hood, pp.25-7.

35.See J.C. Reid, Thomas Hood,p.37. MS Keats House,Hampstead,
16 February 1821.

36.Morgan, The Letters of Thomas Hood, p.22.

37.'The Mary: A Seaside Sketch' in Jerrold, The Collected Poetical
Works, II.42-44, p.628.

38.John Scott (1783-1812) employed at the War Office, afterwards
editor of Drakard's Newspaper, later called The Champion
(1813-16), published volumes of his tours on the continent.
First editor of The London Magazine (1820-2).

39.Reid, Thomas Hood, p. 41.

40.Jerrold, The Collected Poetical Works, Appendix, p. 718.

41.Reid, Thomas Hood, p. 42.

42.Jerrold, The Complete Poetical Works, p. 400. William
    Kitchiner, eccentric, bon viveur, author of The Cook's Oracle
    and works on the art of prolonging life, optics, etc. Editor of
    the sea-songs of Charles Dibdin.

43.Jerrold, The Complete Poetical Works, p. 44.

44.Ibid. 'To a Cold Beauty', p. 182 and 'Sonnet: It is not death',
    p. 194.

45.Morgan, The Letters of Thomas Hood, p. 686.

46.Ibid. p. 65.

47.Charles Wentworth Dilke became Hood's trusted friend and
    adviser, to whom Hood laid bare his soul and mind. To Dilke
    Hood could unburden his most secret sorrows and fears. The
    correspondence during Hood's exile in Germany is particularly
    revealing, much of it being published by Leslie Marchand from
    the Dilke papers in the British Library.

48.John Hamilton Reynolds was Hood's closest friend in the early
    years. He and John Taylor, both of whom were intimates of
    Keats, undoubtedly brought Keats's works to Hood's notice.
    Hood's The Plea of the Midsummer Fairies and Other Poems,
    1827, shows the marked influence of the Keatsian idiom.

49.See P. Thorogood, 'Thomas Hood and the Progress of Cant',
    Papers in Research and Criticism, ed. D. Hawes, Polytechnic
    of Central London, 1978.

50. Sir James Barrie and John Galsworthy later resided in the house, which still stands today, and a plaque records the names of its four famous occupants.

51. Morgan, The Letters of Thomas Hood, p. 71.

52. Ibid. p. 537.

53. W. Jerdan, Autobiography, London, 1852-3, iii. 15-17. William Jerdan was editor of the Literary Gazette (1817-1850). Hood needed his friendship on account of his puffing reviews, but theirs was a friendship that blew hot and cold. In November 1827, Hood reprimanded Jerdan, 'I wrote to you on Friday week, & I have waited daily for your answer, - expecting a cheque on Longman's - which just now would be acceptable'. Later in the same month Hood wrote a rather prickly defence which suggests a rift between the two men, yet in the previous month Hood had made an invitation to Jerdan to dine en famille at Robert Street. A month later, Hood crisply retorted, 'I should never have dreamt of asking for money in advance', (quoted in the Athenaeum 23 July 1892, p. 132 where the rest of the letter is paraphrased, 'Hood has asked Jerdan for an order on Longman's house for payment for three articles. In sending the order Jerdan has assumed that it was "an advance". Hood replied that it was nothing of the kind, the articles having been sent in...' Jerdan endorsed the letter, '... Pettish!.'.') In January 1828 Hood wrote to Charles Tilt, 'I am bored to death by the delay of the Annual Editors - & Jerdan as well' (Morgan, The Letters of Thomas Hood, p. 90). The letters from Hood to Jerdan show an amusing variation in the forms of address:

June 1827 'Dear Jerdan', August 1827 'My dear Jerdan',
October 1827 'Dear Sir' and later in the same month 'Dear
Jerdan'. By March 1829, Jerdan had been restored to favour.
He continued throughout 1831-2 to 'My dear Jerdan' until 4
November 1834 when Hood wrote to complain over a review of
Tylney Hall, when Jerdan is once again demoted 'Dear Sir'.
By 30 December 1844 all was forgiven when Hood wrote to
thank Jerdan for mentioning the pension Hood had been given
(Literary Gazette, 28 December 1844, p.854). Thackeray did
not have a very high opinion of the Literary Gazette, labelling
it 'entirely venal' and referring to Jerdan as 'the puppet of the
booksellers'. See H.G. Hewlitt, Henry Fothergill Chorley,
1873, p.107. In his Autobiography, Jerdan dwelt elaborately
on his financial crises and related his often vicious quarrels
with authors, editors and publishers, presenting himself
invariably as their victim, in a kind of 'apologia pro vita sua',
unable to understand the wiles and guiles of his competitors –
a man, like Hood, far too sensitive for the rough and tumble of
the business world. It seems that Hood was never quite sure
whether Jerdan was to be approached as a friend or foe (i.e.
potential publisher!) and appears to have expected too much
of both. I give this briefest of accounts of a literary friendship
by way of displaying something of that delicate balance that
frequently existed between an author and his editor and publisher.
The story could be told many times over by changing the names.

Jerdan continued to publish a number of pieces by Hood in
the Literary Gazette throughout 1827 including The Demon Ship,
Death's Ramble and The Sub-marine.

54. Hood published several pieces in the pages of Friendship's Offering, including 'I remember, I remember', 'Time, Hope and Memory' and 'I Love Thee'.

55. Morgan, The Letters of Thomas Hood, pp. 75-6.

56. Edward Moxon (1801-58), poet and publisher of Wordsworth, Shelley, Tennyson, Browning and numerous posthumous editions of Hood's works. He married Lamb's protegee, Emma Isola. Worked for Longman (1821-8), then Hurst & Co. (1828-30) where he became friendly with Frederick Mullet Evans, the printer.

57. William Harrison Ainsworth (1805-1882), solicitor who went into the publishing business in London (1826-28). Editor of Bentley's Miscellany (1840-2). Author of thirty-nine novels. Hood, in spite of one or two difficult moments, remained on friendly terms with him. They were both guests at the dinner to welcome Dickens on his return from America on 6 November 1842. Ainsworth was also among the guests at the Hoods' house in St. John's Wood in November 1842. Among others invited were Dickens, Barham, Forster, Sir Charles and Lady Morgan and Manley Hopkins, father of the poet.

58. 'There's No Romance in That' in Jerrold, The Complete Poetical Works, II. 25-8, p. 278.

59. Ibid. p. 35 Epigraph to Whims and Oddities, 1826.

60. Morgan, The Letters of Thomas Hood, p. 55. Marianne Reynolds was Hood's sister-in-law.

61. Robert Stephen Rintoul (1787-1858). The Dundee Advertiser was one of the chief liberal journals in Scotland.

62. Alaric Watts was editor of the Literary Souvenir, to which
    Hood contributed several poems, including 'A Retrospective
    Review'.

63. Morgan, The Letters of Thomas Hood, p. 71, Hood to Watts,
    10 October 1826. Hood had left the paper on 13 August.

64. Hood's modest social background made him rather deferential
    to established figures like Moore and Scott. His excitement at
    the possibility of including such illustrious names among his
    contributors was always offset by the niggling fear that they
    might not deliver the goods, thinking his publications to be
    not quite the thing. He could be playful with Gent and patron-
    ising with Clare, but he always seemed to go cap in hand to
    those greater than himself.

65. Thomas Gent's 'Lines suggested by the Death of the Princess
    Charlotte'. His Poems were published in this year, 1828, and
    included one in praise of Hood. Gent may have contributed a
    piece to The Gem, but nothing appears under his name there.

66. Morgan, The Letters of Thomas Hood, p. 104.

67. Ibid. p. 112.

68. See H. Coleridge, Letters, ed. G. E. and E. L. Griggs, 1936.

69. Morgan, The Letters of Thomas Hood, note to letter from
    Hood to Bradbury, 18 July 1843 and also another letter to
    Bradbury, 19 July 1843.

70. Quoted by Jerdan in his Autobiography, iii. 21.

71. James Silk Buckingham (1789-1855), author and traveller.
    Journalist in London (1824-30). Sheffield M. P. (1832-7). Author
    of autobiography, travels and temperance pamphlets.

72.Charles Wentworth Dilke (1789-1864), antiquary and critic.
Acquainted with Keats and Shelley. Editor of The Athenaeum
(1830-46) (see note 47). Discussed, in The Athenaeum (after
1847), the authorship of The Letters of Junius, seeking to
refute the claim made by John Taylor (see note 17).

73.Allan Cunningham (1784-1842), friend of James Hogg,
secretary to Francis Chantrey, contributed to Blackwood's
Magazine. Hood had first met him when sub-editor of the
London Magazine.

74.Reid, Thomas Hood, p.107.

75.John Wright invited Hood to accompany him to the hunt on Easter
Monday, 1829. Hood wrote, accepting,

> I have never seen a deer, & therefore have never seen
> one hunted... Has a stag any brush that I can bring home
> & make a hearth brush whilst relating the exploits beside
> a winter fire. - I shall come in red with a cap & an
> umbrella which I trust is the Costume - Are pumps
> indispensible? I have no top boots -

Morgan, The Letters of Thomas Hood, p.119.

76.Ibid. p.12.

77.Ibid. p.126.

78.Ibid. p.127.

79.Hood dedicated many of his books to celebrities, including King
William IV, the sixth Duke of Devonshire, the Viscountess
Granville (the Duke's sister) and Sir Francis Freeling and
copies were dispatched to them. The major figures of the day,
both political and literary, frequently purchased or were presented

with copies for their private libraries. A copy that once belonged to Browning (with his bookplate) is part of the author's Thomas Hood Collection.

80. Morgan, The Letters of Thomas Hood, p. 140.

81. The present John Murray once told the author that he had fond memories of taking Hood's Comic Annuals from the shelves of his father's library and chuckling over the woodcuts.

82. See note 53.

83. Morgan, The Letters of Thomas Hood, p. 144.

84. Ibid. pp. 234-5.

85. Since Hood and Lamb lived so close to each other in Islington, few letters between them exist. The author purchased a letter from Lamb to Hood, staying at Brighton - a rare item - for the Thomas Hood Collection some years ago.

86. Morgan, The Letters of Thomas Hood, p. 327.

87. See note 1.

88. Reid, Thomas Hood, p. 132.

89. Charles MacFarlane (d. 1858), traveller in Italy and Turkey, settled in London and devoted himself to literary work in 1829. Nominated a poor brother of the Charterhouse, 1857. His best works were Civil and Military History of England, 8 vols. 1838-44, The Book of Table Talk, 1836 and Reminiscences of a Literary Life, 1857. Hood never mentions him, which indicates that he was not a close friend and places some doubt on the authenticity of his account of Hood's extravagances.

90. Jerrold, The Collected Poetical Works, II. 53-56, p. 244.

91. Letter to Dilke, January 1836 from Coblenz.

92.Jerrold, The Collected Poetical Works, p.186.

93.Quoted from E.E. Sikes, The Greek View of Poetry, London, 1931.

94.Ibid. Aristotle's Poetics.

95.'A Plain Direction' in Jerrold, The Collected Poetical Works, p.538.

Thomas Hood and his publishers: A Checklist

The London Magazine, Baldwin, Cradock and Joy. From 1821
Taylor and Hessey.

Odes and Addresses to Great People, Baldwin, Cradock and Joy,
1825.

Whims and Oddities (1st ser.), Lupton Relfe, 13 Cornhill, 1826.

The Plea of the Midsummer Fairies, Longman, Rees, Orme,
Brown and Green, Paternoster Row, 1827.

Whims and Oddities (2nd ser.), Charles Tilt, 86 Fleet Street,
1827. 2nd ed. published by Hurst Chance & Co., 1829.

National Tales, William H. Ainsworth, Old Bond Street, 1827.

The Gem, William Marshall, 1828.

The Epping Hunt (designs by Cruickshank), Charles Tilt, 86 Fleet
Street, 1829.

Comic Annual, Charles Tilt, 86 Fleet Street, 1831-34.

The Dream of Eugene Aram, Charles Tilt, 86 Fleet Street, 1831.

Comic Annual, A. H. Baily, 83 Cornhill, 1835-39.

Up the Rhine, A. H. Baily, 83 Cornhill, 1839.

Hood's Own, A. H. Baily, 83 Cornhill, 1839.

Tylney Hall, A. H. Baily, 83 Cornhill, 1840 - later published by
R. Bentley.

Comic Annual, Henry Colburn, Great Marlborough Street, 1842.

New Monthly Magazine, Henry Colburn, Great Marlborough
Street, 1843-44.

Whimsicalities, Henry Colburn, Great Marlborough Street, 1844.

Hood's Magazine, H. Renshaw, for the Proprietors, 356 The
Strand, 1844 - published by Edward Moxon after Hood's death

as were most of Hood's works.

Select Bibliography

R. D. Altick, The English Common Reader 1800-1900, 1957.

J. Bauer, 'The London Magazine', Anglistica, University of
  Copenhagen, 1953.

V. Bonham-Carter, Authors by Profession, Society of Authors,
  1978.

G. Bridson and G. Wakeman, A Guide to Nineteenth-Century
  Colour Printers, Plough Press, 1975.

J. Britton, Autobiography, 1850.

T. Chilcott, A Publisher and his Circle: The Life and Work of
  John Taylor, Keats's Publisher, Routledge and Kegan Paul, 1972.

H. Coleridge, Letters, ed. G. E. and E. L. Griggs, 1936.

A. Elliot, Hood in Scotland, James P. Mathew, Dundee, 1885.
  Fasti Ecclesiae Scoticanae, Oliver and Boyd, 1920.

H. G. Hewlitt, Henry Fothergill Chorley, 1873.

D. H. Hawes, 'Thackeray and the Annuals', Ariel, University of
  Calgary, 1976.

Thomas Hood, Collected Works of Thomas Hood, Edward Moxon,
  1869-71.

Thomas Hood, Collected Poetical Works of Thomas Hood, ed.
  W. Jerrold, OUP, 1906.

Thomas Hood, The Letters of Thomas Hood, from the Dilke
  Papers in the British Museum, ed. L. Marchand, Rutgers
  University Press, 1945.

Thomas Hood, The Letters of Thomas Hood, ed. P. F. Morgan,

Oliver & Boyd, 1973.

Tom Hood and F. F. Broderip, Memorials of Thomas Hood,
   Edward Moxon, 1860.

W. Jerdan, Autobiography, 1852-53.

C. MacFarlane, Reminiscences of a Literary Life.

C. A. Prance, The Laughing Philosopher, Villiers Publications,
   1976.

J. C. Reid, Thomas Hood, Routledge and Kegan Paul, 1963.

P. Thorogood, 'Thomas Hood and the Progress of Cant', Papers
   in Research and Criticism, ed. D. Hawes, Polytechnic of
   Central London 1978.